ON TIME

Dr. Carole N. Hildebrand

Balboa Press books may be ordered through booksellers or by contacting:

Balboa Press
A Division of Hay House
1663 Liberty Drive
Bloomington, IN 47403
www.balboapress.com
1 (877) 407-4847

Print information available on the last page.

ISBN: 978-1-5043-6963-3 (sc)
ISBN: 978-1-5043-6965-7 (hc)
ISBN: 978-1-5043-6964-0 (e)

Library of Congress Control Number: 2016919051

Balboa Press rev. date: 12/30/2016

MY OBJECTIVE IN CREATING "ON TIME"

** To take charge of my life

** To organize my life to be able to do more of the things I choose....what I want, where I want, in the comfort and luxury I want, and with the frequency I want...and to do fewer of the things I don't want to do.

To accomplish this objective with greater ease there are three very interrelated elements which I must understand and harmonize.

1. Health
2. Wealth
3. Time

If I have all three in balance, I have the best chance at a self-actualized life...a life of harmony, joy, contribution. Any of the three elements that are limited or missing make life a greater struggle.

Throughout the ages by far the greatest emphasis has been on number two, Wealth, as though, with enough wealth the other two elements can be brought into balance or are even seen as non-essential. But we know that wealth encompasses more than its material manifestation, money. Wealth is a state of mind, an acceptance of abundance. However, if one has material wealth ---without health in mind and body, or without the time to enjoy being with the people you love, doing the things you love---- there is a void that the wealth alone cannot fill. Yet, many lifetimes have been expended in pursuit of wealth to the exclusion of health and time.

In this century man has emphasized health more than in any era in the past, and has doubled longevity...at least in more sophisticated cultures. We might say health is a prerequisite to enjoying access to both wealth and time. Yet, health without wealth and time freedom is of little notice to many. In fact, many people trade their good mental and physical health for wealth, yet are ultimately unable to enjoy that wealth and time without health.

Finally, TIME, the third element, is the most elusive and confusing one to understand; it is something we talk about, think about and refer to constantly—but do not understand. It is at once concrete and abstract. We struggle to deal with it in our **third dimensional world**, yet TIME is a **fourth dimensional concept**, and, therefore, in our daily lives, exists only as an illusion. We have a lot of rules about this illusion. We try to harness it and treat it as though it is real; we try to manage it. **Time cannot be managed, only events can**. We hear people say so often, "I don't have the time", or "I want more time". Therefore in relationship to the quality of our lives as we experience it, an essential distinction is to reveal the elements we refer to as time so they can be understood and directed in such a way that we design our lives to reflect what we value and want. Only in that way can the days of our lives be filled with the people, events, experiences, distinctions, and expansions we seek.

More and more in our complex, information-ridden society we yearn for **time freedom**, an open slate to fill with events that reflect our heart's desires. In essence, then, when people speak of TIME, they speak of choices---choices of perceptions, conscious direction of habits, and events. It is difficult, though, if not impossible, to activate a variety of choices with regularity without **health and wealth**.

Central to these three elements, then, is your consciousness. An **abundance consciousness** directed toward health, wealth, and time will reap all that is sufficient for life. We have made great strides in understanding more about wealth and health. Now it is essential that we shine the light of understanding on this third element of the triumvirate......TIME.

TABLE OF CONTENTS

NOTE: An Action Guide / exercise number is sometimes referenced in the chapters when it is specific to the subject in that Chapter. You may wish to stop reading for a few moments, turn to the end of the book, and take the time to do that particular exercise, before returning to the chapter.

However, it is also a good test of what you recall, or have absorbed, if you wish to wait until you have finished the book, and then do the 32 Action Guide exercises all at once, as a self-examination of what is most important to you about TIME.

INTRODUCTION

Time is precious. The most valuable expenditure you can make in your life is time. It is, therefore, of utmost importance to develop good habits in the use of your time. Take Action. This book endeavors to guide you toward **Time Freedom**.

Time Perception

- Spirit may be timeless, but on this planet, we have agreed on the concept of twenty-four hours in a day. The perception of how slowly or quickly that time elapses depends upon our state of consciousness.
- There is a difference between having the time of your life as a result of a happy event, and having the time in your life, as in owning and directing your time to do the things you want when you want.
- When traveling from one time zone to another, you are simply adopting the habits of that culture for that time, and your momentary perception is the agreement among cultures of a loss or a gain in time.
- Societal context. We think and talk about time all the time. Almost every conversation has many references to time.
- Watches control most of us. We watch the hands move methodically around the circle. Isn't it curious that we watch our watches?

Although our agreements about how to perceive time on this planet are necessary to bring order to our lives, we do not need to let it dominate us. Many of us do, and we stop making it a choice.

North Americans work enormous numbers of hours. We are crazy about time. Is there a cultural misperception about the time it takes to get things accomplished? It could be a genetic, cultural habit because when our ancestors arrived here, there was so much work to do—and there wasn't time to play. Europe is made up of much older countries. They had already developed their infrastructure, roads, transportation, and buildings. When our ancestors arrived on this continent, they had to do that. North Americans got into the habit of working to survive. We got into the habit and never stopped. Now it is a cultural expectation that we accept, without ever questioning its value to us or our culture.

It wasn't so long ago that we thought we would have much more personal time. Thirty-five years ago, they talked about the three-day workweek. We now work seven days per week, running faster than we ever imagined. Do you question why? Some people were frightened by the prospect of a three-day week/five-hour workday, but others were delighted and couldn't wait. Machines, technology, and microchips were going to make it possible. We have all that technology now, communicate halfway round the world in a heartbeat, and get data in a second, but our lives are quite different than projected. We have so much information and stimulation that our brains are having difficulty processing it. Retrieving the right information at the right moment is a challenge.

Our culture has become more frantic. We are doing more things faster, but we are getting things done less effectively. Most programs that seek to help you become more productive do so through organization. Although some of that is helpful, you have to guard against time-consuming management tools that leave you no energy to contemplate how you want to change your consciousness.

You have to manage your attitude and **perception of time** if you want to improve your results. You want to create time consciousness and develop it into a time-abundance consciousness.

We all get the same amount of time. It is what you do with it that matters. People who control their time never do so by accident. They are about results and goals.

An action plan can maximize your outcome. You will be invited in several chapters to explore your own vision of time through the Action Guide workbook of mental exercises, assessing how you use or misuse time in your own life. It can serve as a compass toward time freedom, if you see yourself as a victim of time, guiding you to a more productive view and use of your time.

You may experience upheaval or feel more pressured about how you are using your time. It is like cleaning out a closet. There is a point in the reorganization process when it actually feels less organized. Persistence is critical. To work within a paradigm (your habits and the way you see the world), you have to shift your habits and make big changes. This paradigm-shifting program teaches you to make time work for you.

Chapter 1

THE TIME IN YOUR LIFE

The most valuable expenditure in your life is time. Let your mind wander through ordinary moments that we all experience in our lives and explore the emotions they create.

- Sounds of a hospital, sirens, Lamaze coaching, and babies crying. A voice in the background is saying, "Congratulations, Mr. Smith. It's a girl." ("Isn't She Lovely" by Stevie Wonder is playing in the background).
- Sounds of children laughing at a birthday party and a mother's voice telling the child to blow out the candles.
- Sounds of a grand processional, an authoritative voice giving a speech about proud futures to a graduating class, congratulations and loud cheers from an audience.
- Sounds of people at a wedding.
- Sounds of a cocktail party with clinking glasses and a voice saying, "Congratulations on your promotion."
- A somber nurse saying, "The results of your tests have come in. The doctor would like to see you tomorrow."
- A doctor saying, "I am sorry to report this news. You have only months to live. We suggest you get your affairs in order." (Willie Nelson's "Gee, Ain't It Funny How Time Just Slips Away" is playing in the background)

This is your life. It is precious. Do you perceive and treat it that way? Do you feel time is abundant for you? Do you usually have enough of it to accomplish the things you want to do? Do you rush around, always wishing you had more time to spend with loved ones, work on projects, or enjoy your vacations? Do you tumble into bed at night, reviewing the day's events with a sense of a life well lived and people well loved—or do you force a few hours of sleep so you can compete in another marathon of slavish deadlines?

This is the author, Dr. Carole N. Hildebrand. I want to welcome you to *On Time.* I have designed the exercises in this unique program to guide you through the process of taking charge of the time in your life. Doing this will require a paradigm shift. The way we think about time is important, but we behave as if everything outside of us is in charge.

Most of our behaviors are reactions to events outside of us rather than making our own decisions and taking charge. Most of us behave and feel like victims when it comes to time. Almost everyone feels pressed for time, poor at managing their time, and at fault. Do you know the feeling? This wide-sweeping phenomenon is not a personal one, but the solution is a personal one. The solution is simple. It is not easy, but it is simple. Taking charge of the time in your life requires you to accept responsibility for the time in your life. If that sounds like double-talk, it is not meant to confuse you. As long as we blame events outside ourselves for our feelings, we have not made choices. We are victims.

The way to gain power over anything is to become knowledgeable. Most people are victims of time because they have taken for granted that they have few choices. They rarely question common knowledge about time. People always say they want more time, but there isn't any more time. We all get the same amount of it in a twenty-four-hour day.

Some people use their time more effectively, experience more fun and joy, and get a greater return on their time. They might make more money, but we all get the same amount of the precious stuff. If time is the most precious thing we will ever spend in our lives, why don't we understand it better? There are millions of references to time on the Internet. That is a lot of information, but information is not knowledge. Do not confuse the two. Information is included in knowledge, but it is only part of it. The dictionary says knowledge is the body of truth, information, and principles acquired by mankind. We were taught—from Bible verses, family, or educational leaders to "know the truth, and the truth will set you free." There is only one thing from which to be set free..... and that is ignorance.

This program is about truth and can lead the way to help you take charge of time in your life. I did not say "manage" your time.....TIME CANNOT BE MANAGED. Events can be managed, but NOT TIME. For years, I approached time challenges by looking for solutions. I attended courses, read books, and listened to time management/efficiency experts, but it all fell short of the mark for me. I felt like I was simply rearranging the furniture in the room. In a sense, I had a time-scarcity consciousness that I was always trying to correct.

Time-management systems also focus upon improving scarcity consciousness. This program approaches the solution from the opposite direction. Rather than a system or mechanism to fix time scarcity, we approach time from a consciousness standpoint. The solution rests in the way you think about time. In this book, the goal is to instill **time-abundance consciousness**. This is in harmony with the natural laws of the universe, including the universal mind, where abundance is all-inclusive.

There is only one mind, and when we tune into that universal truth, we see life from the similarities we share rather than from the differences that alienate us. We all know this on a basic level, and when truth is spoken, it resonates with our inner knowing. With time-abundance consciousness, we approach the challenge from the place we want to go, a much more resourceful strategy than avoiding the problem, which is focusing on where we do not want to go.

Let me use a graphic metaphor. Since many of us live our lives like we are racing against the clock, think of a racecar speeding down the track. All of a sudden, the car launches into a terrible spin, turning around and around in circles. How does the driver keep from crashing into the wall? He has to react in an instant—or he will be dead. He keeps his eyes focused on where he is headed-- into the spin. He does not jerk the steering wheel in the opposite direction to avoid the wall. If he does, he will surely smash into the wall. He keeps his eyes pinned on where he wants to go—the direction of the force—and when the energy/speed dissipates enough, he safely changes the direction of his steering wheel or comes to a stop. He can then move forward safely.

The real challenge is focusing during the spin—when fear wants to take over and move in the opposite direction, trying to avoid the wall. That is where knowledge/truth comes in. A professional driver knows he must hold his focus in the spin, no matter what, and he must take congruent action by turning the steering wheel in the direction of his focus. Knowledge is potential. It does not guarantee an outcome unless you take action congruent with it.

Focus on where you are headed—no matter the pressures and fears to the contrary—and take consistent action in alignment with where you want to go. Emerson said, "The only thing that can grow is the thing you give energy to." The great spiritual and philosophical leaders have disagreed about a lot of things, but one thing they universally agree upon is that YOU BECOME WHAT YOU THINK ABOUT. If you want **time freedom**, focus on it. Do not lose yourself in **avoidance-of-time** slavery.

We get what we focus on most. This program will help you focus on time freedom. The exercises will help you identify your beliefs about time (both empowering and limiting). Once you know where you are on a perception scale, you can develop steps to take you where you want to go. This program is a time-freedom compass that points the way.

People use, lose, and abuse time all the time. Schools focus on imparting knowledge, and business courses focus on efficiency. The goal here is to focus on effectiveness. This is heartwarming for effective people. The world is changing at warp speed, and people are getting paid more for what they **do** rather than what they **know**.

The educational process, especially for good students, is the opposite of what is required to make a living in the world. We are taught efficiency, and it is necessary in some circumstances. For example, when I am doing surgery, it is imperative to the outcome of care to be efficient, which includes speed and precision. My challenge is when I use efficiency outside the treatment area. When I apply it to other aspects of my life, it can become ineffective or tyrannical.

Efficiency can be part of effective behavior, but effective behavior does not always include detailed efficiency. You have to remain alert and not turn this time-efficiency concept into a habit where it affects all other aspects of your life. The goal is not to cram more and more activities into a unit of time. The goal is to choose a better activity to accomplish an outcome. Nowhere is this truer than in the world of making a living. *On Time* gives you tools to **earn more money in less time**.

This book is composed of ten powerful chapters that help you identify and organize information about how you deal with time. The time-liberation action guide helps you identify and solve problems, by clarifying them, creating action steps, and taking charge of the time in your life. My goal is to help the reader develop a way of life that will allow you to spend more of your precious moments experiencing the richness you deserve.

I spent many years chasing the elusive dream of better time management. I felt like I was navigating around the challenge of time problems with the wrong map. I could liken the situation to being on a boat in the Delaware River around Philadelphia. I needed a chart of the river, but I was using a map of the streets of Philadelphia. I was in the general vicinity, but I had the wrong tool.

My mentor and friend, Bob Proctor, through his coaching skills as a motivational speaker, helped me identify a classic error. He suggested that I look for solutions outside my habitual way of problem solving. I was attempting to solve my time-pressure problems with time-efficiency solutions because I had been taught that way in my lengthy educational experience.

As I explored my view of time, I began to see my approach to time more clearly. This book and the related action program address the way you think and behave about time. A lot of unconscious, habitual activities are based upon interpretations about time that society has made for generations. Our behaviors and attitudes are so ingrained that most of us have never thought to question or challenge them.

With Bob's encouragement in a coaching program, I began to question and challenge almost everything I had ever thought about time. I realized that most of my thoughts about time came from scarcity and fear. I was a victim of time. Then one day, I made the simple decision to take charge of the time in my life. From that simple declaration of intent, I developed *On Time.* It is my modus operandi. It works for me, and it can work for you.

One of the most effective ways to use the information and teachings in this program is to do the exercises in the time-liberation action guide. You will likely be intrigued and get some value out of the program by reading the chapters, but simply reading it will be an intellectual experience. When you engage in the exercises, you will get the most value and have the best chance of changing your habits into more resourceful ones that will lead you to getting more effective outcomes for the most valuable expenditure in your life. Make your time count.

The greatest benefit of this book is achieved when you take time to just assess your reaction to something posed in the book that strikes you as particularly (or uncomfortably) familiar in your own view of time. You may wish to take time-out from reading to turn to a suggested exercise in the Action Guide, when one is referenced; otherwise, you may choose to wait until you finish reading the book, and then do all of the exercises at once to explore—and compare-- your own way of handling time. There are no right or wrong answers to the questions posted in the exercises in the workbook Action Guide. This will all come together for you as you read the book and are, in various chapters, referred to an individual exercise. Either way, completing the exercises will make you feel more involved in the process of addressing time and its face-to-face meaning in your life. We often get so caught up in right-way or wrong-way of thinking that we become paralyzed and do not even begin. There is no right-way or wrong-way to do anything.

There can be a valid way or a great way, but there is always a better way. The secret to getting ahead is getting started. So keep reading until you are ready to evaluate your own way.

Time-abundance consciousness, our most coveted way, is dealt with in much greater depth later, in chapter 8. If you know where you are, you can create more of what you want. Some things in this program will seem hard to wrap your mind around. You will float in and out of a-ha moments. You will get confused. Lights will go off. I will say something, and you will understand it for a while. Eventually, you will turn a corner and float into confusion. This is a process.

Louise Hay says, "The work you are doing on yourself is not a goal, it is a process—a lifetime process. Enjoy the process."

Time has a relationship to everything in our lives, but we usually do not think or ask questions about it. We accept—without challenge—the things our families and society say about time. We respond in a similar fashion to that of the majority, without asking why. We have underlying anxiety about time. We talk about it constantly, fear it even more, and live in reaction to it. Our response to this anxiety, particularly in North American culture, is to run around like the white rabbit in *Alice in Wonderland*. "I am late. I am late for a very important date... Can't even say good-bye, hello. I am late. I am late. I am late. I am late."

What is time? We are trying to make time logical when it does not really exist. We try to bring order to areas of our lives that do not require it. For example, think about a loved one, a spouse, or a dear friend. Think about doing something you love with that person. Do you have to think about, or worry about having a great time with someone you love? Probably not—if your whole consciousness is in the moment with that person.

In a spiritual context, time just is. It is timeless, infinite, and has no time or space. It is not fast or slow or good or bad. It just is. On this planet, we have agreed on the concept of twenty-four hours in a day to bring order to our perceptions of time. Each of us has different perceptions of time, depending upon our state of consciousness. They can also change, depending upon circumstances.

Time seems to speed up when we are doing things that make us happy, and it drags when we are in pain. We race from one time zone to another when we are in flight. We talk to people halfway around the world where it is a different day. Yet, we all exist in the here and now—in our own experiences. We only experience things in the moment. We take responsibility for time in our lives and direct our thoughts and activities toward it. In the next moment, that moment we just experienced is in the past—and the moment just ahead of us is in the future.

Dreams and plans occur in the delicate balance of focusing on future moments, but we can only execute events in this moment (the here and now). In our consciousness, we skip backward, forward, and to the now in an instant. Plans are developed by projecting thoughts toward the future, thinking or creating something from "no-thing," and bringing it forward to the *now*. We actually create something from nothing. The process of creation can take a few moments or hundreds of years to manifest an outcome.

In a societal context, we think and talk about time all the time. Perhaps it would be more accurate to say we talk about perceiving a lack of time and time pressures all the time. We almost never have conversations that do not relate to something about time. Although our agreements about a context for relating to time on this planet are necessary to bring order to our lives, we do not have to carry it to extremes. Time has taken so much control of our lives that many of us have stopped making choices about time. In fact, many of us do not realize that we have choices about how we deal with time.

North Americans work enormous numbers of hours. We are crazy about time. Professor Carey Cooper, an American at Manchester University in England is one of Europe's foremost stress specialists. He has calculated that the annual cost of stress-related illnesses attributed to overwork tops $80 billion in the United States, which is more than $1,600 per year for every worker. The typical German worker, by comparison, works 320 to 400 fewer hours per year than his or her American counterpart. The average American works eight hours—or the equivalent of one working day—more per week than the average German.

Is there a cultural misperception in North America about the time it takes to get things accomplished? It is a genetic, cultural habit. "Time Pressure in the Nineties," conducted by Hilton Time-Value Surveys, found that 38 percent of the people interviewed reported cutting back on their sleep to make more time, 33 percent said they were unlikely to accomplish what they set out to do each day, and 21 percent said they did not have time for fun anymore. Those pressures have escalated into the twenty-first century.

We have so much information and stimulation that our brains have difficulty processing them. Retrieval of the right information at the right moment is a challenge. On a societal level, we are operating on automatic pilot through time-scarcity consciousness. We developed the habit of working all the time because we needed to survive. Once habits are formed, whether individually or collectively, they drive behaviors. All the gadgets and technology we have ever had—or will ever develop—to save us time will not give us time or time freedom.

We must change our consciousness and our habits about time. Technology could have led to more personal time if we changed how we spend our time. Instead, **we have developed time-saving technology, but an environment of time scarcity, with a survival consciousness**. We have created a feeding frenzy of technology acquisition. It takes time to learn, upgrade, and maintain these tools. It takes money to purchase and constantly change equipment. It takes time to create money. The shelf life of technology is short. It is almost obsolete before it is out of the wrapper.

Less than six hundred years ago, Sir Francis Bacon strove to be a Renaissance man. His goal was to know all the knowledge available at that time. That was a daunting undertaking then, but today it could not even be a wisp of a dream. The volume of new information broadcast and published in every field exceeds anyone's ability to keep pace. More words are published or broadcast in one day than you could possibly ingest in the rest of your life. That information will double again soon.

We have structured our lives around universal tools: cell phones, clocks, and watches. Most of us strap watches to our wrists to help us keep focused. Instead, it becomes a silent slave driver. Many of us live at the mercy of it as the hands move methodically around the circle. Do you not think it is curious? We **watch the watch** so we can meet our deadlines. What a metaphor. A deadline is a line you see on the oscilloscope to indicate that a person's heart stopped beating. No wonder we have negative feelings—or even panic—when we are late. After all, it could mean there is a big penalty for not finishing on time.

Does activity mean productivity? We have become frantic about doing more, faster. We have developed all kinds of aids to theoretically assist in the process of transferring information. We have fax machines, pagers, voice mail, online services of all sorts, and cell phones. There is almost no place at any time we cannot be reached. We wanted access anywhere, anytime; now that we have it, many of us want to screen out all of that access. We have caller ID so we do not have to pick up the phone unless we want to speak to the person on the other end.

By trying to solve our time problems with technology and systems, we have become less productive and less effective. Unfortunately, most of the books, programs, chapters, and seminars that seek to help you become more productive do so through a process of more organizational activities. Although some of that is helpful, you would be wise to guard against time-consuming management tools that leave you no energy for contemplation of how you want to change your consciousness. If you do not fix the way you think about time, all the cyber tools and systems in the world will not fix the feeling that you are on a time treadmill.

When I first became aware that I was a slave to efficiency, I tried to change that dynamic. I needed to understand which behaviors supported effectiveness and which made me ineffective.

Ineffective Activities

- I get sidetracked by other projects in the middle of a current project.
- Since I exercise after all my other activities are completed, I do not get to exercise as regularly as I would like to.
- Since I do not hold personal time sacred, I do not have much uncharted time for spontaneous events with people I love to be with.

Effective Activities

- I plan my day by beginning with visualizations of who I want to become, the home I want to live in, and friends I will be with. I look at the things I want to accomplish and run through them in my mind.
- I keep work orderly and together so I can find things easily. I make retrieval of information easy.
- I pay myself first, before going on any spending sprees, so I always save money regularly.
- I use a company called Moments to keep in touch with my friends. It is a great concept. I made up a list of all the people I want to remember for birthdays, Christmas, Hanukkah, or New Year's Eve.

> Each month, I get cards addressed and stamped for those people. All I have to do is add a personal note and pop them into the mail. I do not leave it to chance that I will have the time to pick up a card individually (or resort to an online greeting). That way, I am able to regularly keep in touch with people I love.

My lists are a lot longer than those examples. When I speak about goals, dreams, or habits, I tend to have broad categories of business life, growth/development (spiritual life), finance, and relationships. I tend to group responses in those major areas of my life.

My effective activities are wins in my life. By constantly visualizing where I want to go, I feel how it will be. I rejoice in the accomplishments I am attracting to my future. I am actually changing my unconscious paradigms to more effective ones. I continue to refine this process. At the beginning of each year, I sit down with my goal sheet. I call it "How Big Can I Dream?" By reviewing what I have written on a monthly basis, I can reinforce effective behaviors that take me closer to my goals. By the end of the year, I can see how much I have accomplished.

We are about to conclude our first module in this program. I have asked you to stretch your mind to encompass a lot of concepts about time because I believe you will find the book more enlightening if you are more in touch with what time means to you. I have asked you to examine and question how we as a culture—and you in particular--- view and feel about time. (You will be able to explore your own view of time when you go to the Time Liberation workbook, Action Guide #1) I have encouraged you to examine the way you think about time and your effective and ineffective behaviors. I have challenged you to change your paradigm and take responsibility for time in your life. By beginning the process of change by choosing one behavior, you will modify or add to your repertoire over the next forty days.

During this time, you will experience upheaval and perhaps feel even pressured about how you are using your time. Habits are not easy to change—even with the best intentions. We only have to look at New Year's resolutions. They often do not last more than the day we dreamed of them . A practical metaphor for this paradigm shift is like reorganizing a closet. Time is like an overstuffed, disorganized closet. You have to deal with it because you need things to run your life. Every time you go in to extricate something from it, boxes fall on your head.

One day, you decide to take responsibility and clean it up. You begin by pulling everything out, examining it, and assessing the relative value of the contents. You discard some items and rearrange others. When everything is on the floor, it looks even more disorganized. You begin to wonder what you have done. Persistence is critical. Dealing with the changes that are necessary to take charge of time is similar to the closet metaphor. There are points in the process when you will feel exhilarated, doubt yourself, or wish you had never started. Hold your focus. Persistence will make you a winner.

Chapter 2

TIME FREEDOM

Explore your associations with the freedom---or lack of--- associated with each of the following:

- In a courtroom, the judge says, "All rise." He pounds the gavel. "This court is now in session."
- A large metal gate clangs shut. One prisoner whispers to another, "Hey, Joe. What you gonna dream about tonight?" A dejected voice sighs and replies, "Aw, same old, same old."
- Janice Joplin sings "Bobby McGee." "Freedom's just another word for nothing left to lose."
- A mother talks quietly to a child as she puts her to bed, the child giggling. The mother says, "Sara, what are you going to do tomorrow?" The child says, "Grandma's going to pick me up; we are going to the playground, and we are going to Jane's house to get my new puppy." The mother says, "Good night, darling. Have wonderful dreams tonight. Tomorrow's going to be so exciting for you."
- The sound of fireworks, loud voices, and cheering at an event.

Webster defines **freedom** as **absence of necessity, coercion, or constraint** in choice or action. This concept applies to money as well. Financial freedom is possessing the resources to do anything you want, as much as you want, anytime you want, for as long as you want (provided it does not infringe on the rights of others). This concept applies to time. Time freedom is that state of acceptance of responsibility about time emanating out of a time-abundance consciousness in which one chooses attitudes and activities about time. Attitude is comprised of thoughts, feelings, and actions.

Hello, this is Dr. Hildebrand again. I want to welcome you to the second chapter. In chapter 1, we talked about time-abundance consciousness and taking responsibility for the time in your life. We will expand on both concepts in future chapters. They are foundations of consciousness and make the paradigm shift necessary to move from time slavery to time freedom. This transition can be a joyous journey, a laborious effort, or an impossible obstacle. Which will it be for you? Your mind will latch onto one of the choices instantly. That is likely your habitual mind-set for how you approach change.

It is important for you to be aware of the inherent changes we all face because we live in a culture and an era like no other. Perhaps the only certainty upon which we can count is that there will be persistent, pervasive, and rapid change. For technologically advanced countries, this process is moving at breakneck speed. Your mind-set is about change. You can work with it. It is important to know where you are so that your strategies moving forward can be structured to deal with your current mind-set. If you are more rigid and fearful about change, you can embrace it with a more adventuresome spirit.

This is a paradigm-shifting program. A paradigm is a philosophical framework with theories, laws, and generalizations to support that context. A paradigm that many of us have is that time is scarce. If I have that paradigm operating inside me, I relate everything concerning time to that context. I wake up in the morning and think about all the things I have to do. I feel frantic that I will never complete them all. I look at the clock at three o'clock and say, "There are only a few more hours until dark." I look at a week's vacation on the horizon and think it is not enough time to do much of anything. I wish I had more time.

If I come from a paradigm of time being abundant, those three events would invoke a different set of thoughts and reactions. I will awake in the morning, thinking of the day as a whole expanse of time ahead of me to accomplish a lot. I think of how I will organize myself to accomplish all the things I have to complete. I think about the steps I could take to accomplish several of my tasks simultaneously. I think of who I can get to help me. I look at the clock at three o'clock and think, *I have three more hours before it gets dark.* I anticipate the week's vacation coming up and think about all the adventures I am going to have and all the moments I am going to have to reconnect on a deeper level with people I love. My thoughts will be on appreciating living at a time when I have so many conveniences and so many options.

The paradigm within which we work personally, our family, has established a culture. The society we live in has adopted our contexts over the generations. We are actively aware of some of them, and we are totally on automatic pilot with others. We have plenty of habits that we do repetitively and never question. Paradigms are habits—whether individual or cultural—and they operate simultaneously. They sometimes harmonize with one another or conflict with one another.

To understand how to change anything, it is important to understand your habits, how they are formed, and how you can change them. **If you manage your habits, you manage your results. If you manage your results, you manage your destiny.**

To understand how habits are formed, imagine your mind. If you are having trouble doing that, let me suggest the **stick person concept**, which was developed by Dr. Thurman Fleet in the 1930s and introduced to me by motivational speaker, Bob Proctor. (It is explored fully in the workbook, beginning with Action guides #11 - #14.) When you truly understand and integrate the stick person concept into your life, a wonderful world of power, possibility, and promise will open for you.

To bring order and understanding to your mind, you need an image. We think in images and pictures. Confusion is usually the result of not being able to clearly image an idea. Since your mind is part of your personality, you must engage your imagination to build this image. Visualize your head as your mind, and everything from your neck down as your body. The mind is energy. The mind is movement. The mind is in every cell of your body, and the body is the manifestation of that movement called mind.

The body is nothing but an instrument of the mind. Visualize the top half of your head as being your conscious mind and the bottom half of your head as the subconscious mind. Assume for a moment that every bodily movement you make is motivated by your mind. We think in pictures or images. If you think of a watch, a picture of a watch flashes on the screen of your mind. The stick person gives you a graphic illustration of the three parts of your personality.

Throughout history, the most elegant solutions to universal questions are often simple. They are not necessarily easy. The stick person concept is built upon the premise that you have a power within you that is far superior to any condition or circumstance around you. With free will, your thoughts can direct this power to whatever results you choose in this lifetime.

You have a power within you that is far superior to any condition or circumstance around you. If you have not consistently tapped into this truth, your happiness, sorrow, and apprehension are likely responses to circumstances around you. If you win a beautiful compass at a charity event, you are happy. If you are late for an important meeting because of an accident on the expressway, you are frightened and unhappy. You are being controlled by the circumstances outside yourself. You have a greater power within, but most of us fail to consciously use that power to direct ourselves. By understanding how our minds work, we can shift habits and modify our behaviors to more resourceful ones.

With the stick person, the conscious mind is the part of your personality that thinks and reasons. Your free will lies there. That part of your mind decides how much money you want to earn and how much leisure time you want to have. The conscious mind is able to accept or reject any idea. Thoughts come into your conscious mind actively and passively. You generate active thoughts. Passive thoughts are generated by someone or something outside yourself. They are taken in unconsciously and uncritically when you have shut down your screening process.

When you are tired, you are not consciously directing your thoughts. Be aware that no person or circumstance can cause you to think about thoughts or ideas you do not actively choose. Allow your mind to be an open channel to information from outside your own thoughts. Information can come into your mind passively when your consciousness is drifting—in front of the TV, with a conversation or the radio in the background. The thoughts you choose eventually determine the results in your life. Pain, pleasure, and limitation originate in the conscious mind through our own thoughts or are passively accepted from outside sources.

When you were a child, all the things your parents said to you programmed your subconscious mind. You accepted them automatically. When you grew up, you began to question some of the things you believed. Maybe they told you money is evil or life is a treadmill. You might have accepted that without challenging the thoughts from your parents.

When you are not focusing your thoughts, you take in information from the TV, people around you, and headlines in the newspaper. These thoughts are transferred to your subconscious when you are on automatic pilot. As you accept thoughts consciously or unconsciously, they are impressed upon your subconscious mind.

The subconscious mind is the most magnificent part of who you are. It is the power center. It functions in every cell of your body. Every thought your conscious mind chooses to accept—actively or passively—the subconscious mind automatically accepts. In fact, it has no ability to reject. It knows no limits except those you consciously choose. The subconscious mind functions voluntarily—whether you make any effort to influence it or not. The subconscious mind will not remain idle. It will feed upon the thoughts you generate and those you reach as a result of neglect.

All thought impulses that get through the screen of the conscious mind are accepted automatically by the subconscious mind. You have continuous thoughts. You cannot entirely control your subconscious mind, but you can voluntarily hand over to it any plan, desire, or purpose you wish transmitted into concrete form. Any conscious or unconscious thought you repeatedly impress upon your subconscious mind becomes fixed in your subconscious. That is a very important point because fixed concepts are habits. Once habits are formed, you automatically behave in alignment with those thoughts (without consciously thinking about them). If you do not like the results you are getting in your life, you can change your subconscious programs or habits for a more desired outcome.

The body is the most obvious part of you, but it is the smallest part. The body is the physical presentation of you. The material medium is just an instrument of the mind. Your body is the house in which you live. The thoughts and images you consciously choose, especially if they are repetitive, are impressed on the subconscious. They are in every cell of your body. When your body moves into action, your actions determine your results.

If you have all **three parts in harmony**—the **conscious**, **subconscious**, and the **body**—you will get more of what you want. Managing your mind will manage your results. In this book, you will learn how to utilize it in context to the **time in your life**.

Behavior is controlled by the subconscious mind. Not all our behaviors are resourceful and effective, and when we consciously acknowledge that we want to change a behavior, it can be a real challenge. It depends upon how ingrained the behavior is in your consciousness. If it is something you have believed and acted on the whole of your life, passed down through the culture and your family, or heavily reinforced, it can take courage, commitment, and persistence to change your thoughts and behaviors.

If you are trying to break a bad habit like smoking, you will automatically replace it with another bad habit unless you consciously replace it with a good habit. This is because nature abhors a vacuum, and it automatically rushes in to fill the space that is vacated. If smoking is a non-resourceful habit, you will automatically replace it with another non-resourceful habit unless you consciously plan to replace it with something that supports you. The consciousness that would be most resourceful in this case would be developing habits that support health. Focus on your health. When you want to smoke, take a walk, read a passage in a book, or listen to a few moments of a chapter that focuses on habits that support health. Decide what your options will be in advance. Don't try to think about what you can do to get your mind off the cigarettes when you feel the craving.

When you are under the gun of physiological and habitual behavior patterns, it is not the best environment to choose a more resourceful behavior. Decide in advance and automatically go do it the minute those pangs strike. Mentally focus on what you want. Let us play a mental game for a moment. Are you ready? Do not think about a clock. (What just happened? An image of a clock flashed on the screen of your mind.) When people say, "I am not going to think about smoking," guess what they're thinking about? People who consistently manage their behaviors by **focusing on what they want—rather than trying to resist what they do not want**—change their destinies.

When it comes to change, you will never seriously desire something you are not capable of accomplishing. (You can check your association to change in Action Guide #15). There is some kind of genetic governor that will not permit us to seriously entertain an idea we are incapable of manifesting. How much energy, focus, and repetition do we have to employ? <u>As much as it takes</u>.

To shift something you recently developed takes a little effort. Shifting a lifelong habit that has been reinforced through society over the generations can take a lot of repetitive reinforcement. If you have a good attitude about change and constantly reinforce those attitudes by flexing your change muscles, you will be able to tackle change regularly with more versatility. If you huddle in the corner with steadfast resolve, change will be a formidable mountain to climb. The only certainty we can count on is that we are living in an era of change. Doesn't it make sense to test yourself regularly so you can be ready for changes as they propel toward you?

With any change, there will be uncertainty. The vibration in your body when you are uncertain can be excitement or fear. The interpretation you make about that feeling will be resourceful (excitement) or non-resourceful (fear). Use your conscious mind to hold the thoughts you want to entertain and the outcomes you want to achieve. We call this crossing the **terror barrier** (Action Guide #15). The bigger the change—and the more awesome the terror barrier—the greater the resistance.

You can move through the terror barrier by holding your thoughts on your desired goal—rather than using your current results as your gauge of the future—trusting in yourself as a part of divine substance, and constantly taking action toward your goal. You can change your old paradigm. The more changes you want to make, the more terror barriers you will face. And you will face them again and again and again. Each time you face them and move forward, you grow your "change muscles".

It is not as though you have one terror barrier per item. Each time you face it, you feel stronger. I used to have a phobia of heights. I live on the seventeenth floor of a high rise-building. When I walked out on my balcony, I would have sweaty palms, my stomach would turn, and my knees would weaken. I would clutch the railing and drop down to the floor when I got closer to the edge.

As a part of a growth training I participated in several years ago to face my fears, I climbed a fifty-two-foot telephone pole. I did not elegantly race up that pole. I hugged that pole like I was one with it. The only way I could keep moving was to focus on getting to the top. About halfway up, I looked down and felt sheer terror. I was frozen with fear. **It was a terror barrier**. The only way to continue was to look up. I forced myself to focus on where I wanted to go. I fixed my eyes on the top and inched my way up.

When I go out on my balcony, I still have flutters, but I do not clutch the railing and drop to my knees. I have diminished my resistance to height. I could further diminish it by doing activities that would challenge that fear. I could take up mountain climbing or skydiving. If it were important enough to become totally comfortable with heights, I know that—with enough focus, repetition, challenge, and moving through my terror barrier—I could change that paradigm. That particular paradigm, however, is not so limiting that it keeps me from doing things I love.

I focus on other terror barriers with regularity. For you, it could be confronting your boss or public speaking. For anything you can imagine, the process is the same. The energy one is willing to devote to shifting a paradigm is directly related to the importance one places on the new paradigm. If it is something that you would like to change, but it doesn't represent a burning need, you won't confront the terror barrier on that issue with enough regularity and intensity to banish it completely. Each time you do, you will diminish it as an obstacle. The secret to removing terror barriers with regularity is to elevate the thing you want to change from a want to a must. We flirt with our wants. We accomplish our musts—no matter how long they take.

If you have a rough time with change, focus on one or two things you want to shift at a time. If your focus is constantly shifting from one event to another, you will be challenged without direction. You will have more difficulty reaching your new paradigm. Depending upon its importance in your life, it might take singular focus for a critical paradigm shift. We change our subconscious programs through repetition of a new thought. The more frequently you can focus on the new thought while you are emotionally involved with the new idea, the faster you will change the paradigm. Once changed, the new behavior has to be reinforced regularly to be sustained.

Moving toward time freedom for most of us is a major paradigm shift. What you choose to do with time freedom once you have created more of it will vary greatly from one person to another. Some people want to luxuriate more. Some people want to explore more or learn more. Some people want to be of more service. Some people want to create more or work more on something they love. Some people love to work, but they do not get to work enough on the things they love. One man's way of expressing how he allocates his time ideally will be the exact opposite for someone else. Be careful not to weigh someone else's use of time with your finger on the scale.

Look through your frame of references and your paradigms. Don't judge someone else's choices based upon your goals, which can be very misleading. It is important to clarify what you want to do when you have time freedom.

In general, our judgments of events get in the way of joy. Our particular frame of reference or the glasses through which we see the world is a box. That is our paradigm. We usually operate from inside the box. When we want to change something, we rearrange the furniture inside the box by doing something differently. By doing something differently often enough—with sheer force of will—you can change a habit. If you really want the change to last, you have to get outside the box to where freedom exists. By shifting the way you think consistently and taking action from that place, you are operating out of the box. The key to winning back your time is to be more effective at "being" rather than "doing".

When we are being, rather than doing, we see time as it really is-- **It just is**. It is not good or bad or fast or slow. In fact, every event just is. In our attempts to label and categorize those events, we judge them rather than simply noticing them from a neutral place.

Our perception of time changes dramatically depending upon our connectedness to the events that are happening. Time races when we are doing things we love with people we love, and it drags when we are doing things we do not enjoy with people for whom we have no affinity. We perceive intense events that are happening on either end of the spectrum. When events are very positive, time races. When they are very negative, time drags. The goal is to stay consciously connected in the moment, each and every moment. The more one can do that, the more one is operating from freedom and able to create more effective outcomes in relationships, business, sports, or other events.

This moment is the only one upon that we can truly have any impact. Most people fail to stay connected except in extreme moments. Action can only be taken in this moment. That is why this moment is your only point of power. There is no potency in spending too much time in future dreaming except to identify and structure your direction as one would use a compass. In reminiscing about the past, identify what you can use for today's work. You will perceive more value when you stay consciously connected in the moment. In that perception, we have the opportunity to manage our outcomes more effectively. Get more of the experience we seek more consistently.

Children have an easier time staying consciously connected in the moment. They are alert to all that is going on around them and are less distracted. Their perception of time is quite different from an adult's perception.

When we were young, two important distinctions about our time perception were operating. First, when our mothers told us to be patient, we just had to wait until tomorrow for grandmother's arrival, she was talking about a day and a night. Even if we were too young to conceptualize twenty-four hours in a day, it was a huge span of time. As we got older, twenty-four hours wasn't so much. If you speak to the elderly, they perceive that same twenty-four hours as a blink of an eye. When we are young, time looms ahead of us. We are less conscious of the fact that each of us has a finite number of moments to spend. The young undervalue moments.

In society, we scurry around from one event to another, often without taking a breath in between. Many times, we do not even perceive the events themselves; we perceive our time constraints and the need to rush to the next event. Keeping track of time, rather than experiencing events, takes up almost all of our consciousness. By being involved with time rather than the event, we miss being in that moment, the act of doing whatever it is. And we miss joy.

We tend to hurry more when we fail to plan effectively. Part of effective planning can have an efficiency component, but most of us confuse the two concepts and interchange them in our thoughts and in our actions. Many people think effective is efficient. The first question you should always ask yourself about anything is why not how. We are such an action-oriented culture that one of our chronic habits is going automatically to the process of solution, bypassing the inquiry stage.

I am not suggesting that you ponder every potential event for hours. If you do that, you won't have time to take action, and **action is the highest form of affirmation**. Remain more alert in general. With events propelling toward you at breakneck speed, you need to hone your reactions to immediately exclude those events that do not take you closer to your goals. It is much more difficult, time-consuming, and ineffective to do something without thinking. Don't take on another commitment or task only to find that you have expended a great deal of energy on something that is a low-to-no-priority event in your busy life.

I am a person who loves order. I like things organized, neatly away in file folders or in books. The minute I look at my mail, I want a logical place to file the information. When I go on automatic pilot, I avoid my first question of why does it have to be done. I automatically go into the process of neatly filing the material away. Even if I have someone else do it, like my life coordinator, I still might file something away that I will never use. Beautiful orderly files of information I will never use are not effective, and the time was wasted. The time to sift through it later, only to delete it, is doubly ineffective.

Chapter 5 details effective versus ineffective behaviors and makes even more refined distinctions between effective and efficient activities. Effective action includes planning. A plan gives us confidence, and from that solid foundation, we can be more flexible and versatile in our responses to unexpected events. The element of time pressure alters behavior, attitudes, and physiological responses.

Subjective time can be an incredible, powerful force. It is no accident that the word deadline contains the word dead. As more devices have arisen to conserve time, and more activities deemed crucial to achieving a balanced existence have been identified, people have begun to fill their newly saved time more rapidly than additional time can be minted. We perceive ourselves as victims of time.

Time freedom rests in taking responsibility for the time in our lives. If we feel, speak, and believe from a time victim's box, we never seem to get enough time—no matter how many people we employ to help, no matter how much time-saving technology we purchase, and no matter how many methods of efficiency we learn. We never seem to get enough time. When we take responsibility for how we invest and spend our time, the time victimization box disappears.

Time freedom is responsible, or the ability to respond. My friend, Bob Proctor, never wears a watch. He has taken ultimate responsibility for time in his life. He has trained his mind to be aware of time, and his brain tunes into that. If you see the value of developing time-abundance consciousness with time freedom as your goal, are you still living in the time victim's box? (You can explore your TIME FREEDOM attitude in Action guide #17).

When will you enable yourself to take charge of time in your life?

Chapter 3

A SENSE OF URGENCY

After reading each of these announcements, close your eyes for a moment and tune in to the emotions each one elicits:

- Voice of a reporter giving a weather forecast with a hurricane or tornado ready to hit. There is a sense of alarm in his voice as he talks about evacuating the area.
- Soundtrack of a World War II movie inside an airplane under attack. The pilot is talking to base about the hit his plane has taken. He tells his men they must bail out (noise and scurrying as the plane door opens).
- Professor speaking to a college class about upcoming national board examinations, encouraging them to study intently every day. It's an opportunity to pull together all they have learned in the past four years. Passing it will determine if they can practice medicine. Most people cannot do well if they wait until the end to pull it together. The volume of information to review is too great. Do not leave it to chance. Review everything. Be thoroughly prepared.
- Soundtrack to *Dead Poets Society,* and Robin Williams says, "Carpe diem" (seize the day).

Nothing makes a person more productive than **the last minute**. Why do you suppose that is? It is because of the **sense of urgency** inherent in the last minute.

Hello, this is Dr. Hildebrand again, and I want to welcome you to chapter 3.

Many people misperceive what a sense of urgency means and interpret it as panic. It is, in fact, the opposite—provided one's emotional state is focused in a calm, confident, relaxed fashion. We can actually apply the effectiveness of the last-minute advantage by using a sense of urgency with anticipation of the overriding emotional state instead of the tension that many people apply. An effective sense of urgency creates a feeling that keeps you focused. There are so many events and distractions today that one could constantly be in motion and accomplish very little. A sense of urgency used in a resourceful way can help you focus your energy and cut through a lot of extraneous information. It will direct you toward resolution and solution by a quicker route.

A sense of urgency is a quality that you either inherently have or do not have. It is like having a pleasant personality. Some people are do-ers. Do-ers have an automatic sense of urgency. In fact, if you have ever participated on a project with a group, whether it is sports, a work project, or a fund-raising event for a charitable organization, you might have noticed that 80 percent of the effort is performed by 20 percent of the people. These 20 percent are the do-ers, and they have an inborn sense of urgency. They understand the goal is completion and getting ahead means getting started right away with a plan—and working on it regularly and diligently. They use momentum to its full advantage.

We define a sense of urgency as being able to automatically detect projects that achieve goals and work on them routinely until they are successfully completed. If you do not have an innate sense of urgency, you can develop it consciously and deliberately. All it takes is the discipline to follow through. Your sense of urgency will always be in direct ratio to your commitment to results, particularly as it relates to specific projects. Developing a sense of urgency into a habit is a project in itself. It is a very worthwhile investment of your time. It will add power to your repertoire of behaviors and make you a desirable addition to any effort.

The world has always cried out for men and women who can get things done and see a task through to completion. These producers of the world change the world's standard of living. Millions of people are held back from success because they do not know how to get things done. The biggest handicap to success is weakness.

People who fail to make their lives great know what to do, and they almost do it on time. They almost get promotions. They almost become leaders. They **almost** make it, but miss by a minute or a month, but they do miss. They never properly develop a sense of urgency.

The "almosts" are not lazy. Often they are busier than the effective few. They often putter around all day long and half the night, but they fail to accomplish tasks of importance. They are frequently held back by indecision, lack of organization, and paying too much attention to minor details. They shift their focus frequently rather than targeting a specific goal, chart a straight course toward it, and stick to it no matter what.

The **producers** are those people who have fine-tuned their sense of urgency for getting things done, and they will not permit the almosts to distract them. They raise the world's standard of living, and they win the big share of the world's rewards. Producers understand the law of cause and effect. There is no such thing as service without reward. They understand how it applies to everything in life. The law of cause and effect (Action Guide 20) applied to your livelihood is known as the law of compensation, and it is in direct ratio to:

- the <u>need</u> for what you do
- your <u>ability</u> to do it
- the difficulty there will be in <u>replacing you</u>

Try to become more effective and professional every day in every way, and you will find that the need for what you do, as well as the difficulty in replacing you, are automatically taken care of.

People who have developed a time-abundance consciousness are often the producers of the world, and they learned that you do not necessarily have to slow down. You have to learn to calm down. They know how to use a sense of urgency in a relaxed manner to shift the energy of the last-minute advantage from one of tension to precise behavior. They are able to automatically detect projects that are goal-achieving activities and work on them routinely. They understand that the brain and heart resonate with things that make a difference.

The objective of an effective person is not being busy, but it could be part of your old paradigm. It has to be effective. You might be busy in the process of being effective, but it depends upon your goals. It is not the number of things you do; it is the effectiveness of each act that counts. In fact, the more things you do, the worse it will be for you if all your acts are ineffective. The cause of failure is doing too many things in an ineffective manner and not enough things in an effective manner. Every act is a success if it is an effective one, and the sum of a life of effective acts is a successful life. When every action you take is strong, efficient, and effective—by using your willpower to hold the vision of your desired outcome while you are taking action and putting your whole faith, expectancy, and purpose into it—you have a formula for being successful.

In *The Science of Getting Rich,* Wallace Wattles says, "You can make each act a success because you have supreme power with you (some call it universal mind, the source, God)...but whatever your supreme power, it is with you, and never fails." Wattles speaks of getting rich as being a science just like mathematics. His book is a rich resource for abundance consciousness.

To be effective, it is important to stay conscious of goal-achieving activities. As Cyril Northcote Parkinson said, work expands to fill the time available for its completion. Because of this phenomenon, it is easy to use up little pockets of time, which, if directed with more clear intention toward a specific goal, could bring you closer to your big dream. It is amazing how five minutes wasted here and there all day adds up to an hour. Just one hour per day every day for one year adds up to the equivalent of nine full weeks of work (nine forty-hour weeks). It is the principal of compounding at work. We tend to associate this principal with money, but it is equally true for time. At first glance, five minutes seems like very little time to accomplish anything. Even the accumulation of twelve five-minute increments into one hour does not seem to have much impact, but one hour per day for one year adds up to a lot (nine forty-hour weeks). Once anything reaches critical mass, the cumulative effect has extraordinary momentum. This is true in resourceful and non-resourceful directions.

"Do you have a minute?" A seemingly innocent request from an associate can be deceiving. The dynamic that is about to take place has been repeated in millions of offices across the country every day. Often this minute is more like fifteen to forty minutes of your time, and it is more often than not a request to voice a complaint. What is your time worth? *There are a half million minutes in a year. A half million is a lot. I can afford several of them for a colleague.* The truth is you often do not even question the cost of your time. You do not set limits. Many times, you go on automatic pilot. If someone makes a request, you genuinely want to help and say yes before thinking about what you're prepared to give. Your time becomes open-ended.

Do you think to treat every minute like it is precious—or do you treat a lot of them habitually and unconsciously like they are throwaways? I believe people and relationships are important. I want to be emotionally accessible, but I also want to take responsibility for the quality of my interactions and the time I devote to them. A way to be accessible and responsible at the same time is to surround your "yes" response with clear limits. *I'm interested in what you have to say, Joe, but I have a deadline on a project. I have a client I agreed to call in five minutes. What's the general topic?* That gives the other person an opportunity to weigh whether it is important to talk to you at that very moment. It gives you an opportunity to assess from their tone of voice, body language, and topic, if it is something you want to deal with right then. If it is something you need to know or want to help with, you have set a limit up front. You have expressed a time constraint.

If you sense that you will need more time, it gives you a chance to reschedule the conversation for a time that works better for you. The meta message you have conveyed is that the person is important and you care about what he or she has to say. You have to value your own time. If their purpose was just to voice a complaint, they will have their needs met by the next person who allows the conversation without guidelines. If it is something you can genuinely help with, you will have structured a better strategy. You will have managed to net a more effective use of your time around that event. (Explore your reaction in Action Guide #23)

Remain conscious of how you invest your moments. When you spend your time doing anything, it is actually an investment in that event. You can focus on a more finite outcome. If you begin to view your life as a series of connected events, you can weave the fabric of your life into a quilt of rare quality. We often disassociate events in our minds and treat them as standalone moments. We fail to use the principal of compounding time in the most effective way.

People frequently overestimate what they can accomplish in one year because they are impatient for results. They usually underestimate what they can accomplish in five years because they do not exercise persistence toward a designated goal. Using investment in the stock market as a metaphor, consider the fact that many people fail to have plans for investment with designated portions for income and dividends, percentages for long-term appreciation, and lesser amounts to risk for short-term speculation.

By failing to have a plan, or not working it diligently, you are setting yourself up for diminished outcomes. Assume you are at a cocktail party with someone who appears to have a better inside track and talks about a hot tip to make you rich. You perceive this person as more knowledgeable than you. You give up your power immediately. The first chance you can, you call your broker and buy the stock. Over the ensuing months, the stock descends. You double up your investment to average down. When you cannot deal with the pressure anymore, you feel totally out of control. You sell at a loss.

Three years later, the stock price has tripled. Had you investigated the hot tip in more detail to see how it might fit your overall investment strategy, you might have decided to purchase it anyhow. If you examine the fundamentals of the company and consider it a worthwhile risk, you constantly reassess your reasons for having it. If it meets your criteria, continue to hold it through downturns.

To be an effective goal achiever, it is helpful to define your outcome in advance and constantly reassess your decisions based upon the destined outcome. Isolated events will change, which can cause you to modify your strategy, but jumping from one event and strategy to another with little persistence of focus is ineffective. Effective people analyze and reach decisions quickly, but they change their strategies very little. The secret is persistence, and it is a key element of effective behavior and outcomes.

The reason people overestimate what they can accomplish in one year and underestimate what they can accomplish in five years is they have not selected strategies of behavior consistent with their goals. Goal-achieving activities have failed to persist. Five years of persistent, consistent energy and action toward a planned outcome is bound to compound your results. The same energy bouncing from one focus to another is far less likely to lead to an effective outcome.

There is an entire process of defining, identifying, and clarifying your goals based upon your values. Set up a working strategy to concentrate on your highest-priority goals in chapter 4. Once you have identified several of your highest-priority goals, you need to commit yourself to taking action on them daily.

Goal-achieving activities are based upon developing effective habits, and part of that process is working consistently every day—even a little bit at a time—on this new habit or project. For most of us, it is best to focus on one or two modifications or changes at a time. Do not overload yourself. You want to set yourself up to have a lot of wins. This will reinforce the benefits of continuing. By working a bit each day on a project, you make it a less intimidating task.

A lot of what we are willing to tackle has to do with how we manage our perceptions. One of the reasons we resist adding a new project or working regularly on shifting a habit or adding a more resourceful habit to our daily activities is we perceive it will take too much time. A neat way to reduce your resistance to adding that new habit or project and not feel overwhelmed about it is Hashem Khosrovani's rule of 48. (Action guide #25)

If you view a day as being comprised of forty-eight half-hour increments and set aside 2/48 of a day to handle a new project, you have already determined that you see value in what seems like a small stretch. It's not such an overwhelming thing to do. What you are doing with this perceptual shift is diminishing your resistance, making its completion seem much more possible.

Our perceptions help dictate our willingness to do or not do something. Finding ways to maneuver our perceptions to support something valuable is a helpful lifelong strategy. For example, people who do not have the habit of spending less than they earn think they cannot begin to save money until they have real money to save—and they never get started.

If you just saved the twenty dollars a week that many of us spend unthinkingly, and unnecessarily, throughout a working career between the ages of twenty and sixty, you would start retirement with almost an extra $41,000, maybe more, if you were adding it to a retirement investment account. (The amount may not look impressive for facing retirement, but it is a nice bundle created from money that might otherwise have been spent mindlessly.) The point is about what TIME can do even with small amounts of money. But because our perception (or misperception) is that you need a lot of excess money on hand to make any real difference, most people never understand that getting ahead is getting started—with money, careers, and projects.

In the United States the sad truth is that only 5 percent of the people, after they cease their jobs, are economically prepared to live as they did when they worked. Almost everyone could be doing so if they shifted their perceptions and developed regular saving habits. That is not such a burdensome shift to make, yet millions of Americans will live much less well in their after-work years because they failed to make this subtle distinction early enough. If you start young enough, time works greatly in your favor—and you do not have to have large dollars to end up secure, if not well-off. To emphasize the **importance of time**, using the example just given, if you started saving just ten years later, at age thirty, you would have to save around $27 weekly, and if starting at age 40, of course you would have to save double the money, $40 weekly, to net the same amount by age sixty. Perhaps you dismiss the idea by thinking it would be easier to save larger amounts when you are older? "Perhaps not", if you consider various unknowns, such as children, education, health issues, etc. In every instance, on the other hand, the principal of **compounding your time and money** adds awesome strength and more options to your life.

A little later in the program, we will be dealing with identifying resourceful perceptions that support your expansion and the perceptions that inhibit your progression. We will deal very specifically with decisions in chapter 4 and setting priorities in chapter 5. To better deal with the time in our lives, most of us will require a paradigm shift. For some, it will be a minor adjustment, and for others, it will be a life-defining experience.

A paradigm shift is nothing more than a shift in habits. And even if the shift is relatively minor, it gets uncomfortable. We will deal in much greater detail with your paradigm shift in chapter 4. Having a good idea about what to expect during such times is important. It is your compass that keeps pointing you in the direction of a fuller and more effective life. Both decision-making and priority setting are intimately related to a sense of urgency. To feel a compelling drive with ever-changing targets will expend a lot of energy, but it will not necessarily result in an effective outcome. Effective outcomes are very much related to the decisions you make, your goals and priorities, persistent work, and focus. Any new habit will require a great deal of energy, focus, and persistence to begin to effectively impact your subconscious mind. Over time, as you build momentum, it will take decreasing amounts of energy to sustain the change.

Momentum is a physical property in which mass and motion equal the velocity. The bigger the size, once in motion, the faster the object will move. When momentum is applied to ideas, projects, and habits, the properties are the same. A big idea starts out small; as you add focus and persistence, it grows. As it grows, it picks up steam. It takes progressively less energy to keep it in motion, but if you keep adding energy, once it has achieved critical mass, the speed accelerates with almost no effort.

At work with momentum are several laws of physics: first, energy at rest tends to remain at rest, and energy in motion tends to remain in motion. Second, it takes far more energy to activate a change than to sustain a change of state. When we look at any of our existing habits, whether they were activated consciously or unconsciously, they were impressed on the subconscious mind. The more repetition in our hearing and acting upon those programs, the more strength those habits took on. In other words, recently acquired habits usually have less momentum and are easier to disrupt. The modification of that general phenomenon rests with emotional intensity.

A habit, like a phobia, can develop almost instantly without multiple episodes of reinforcement if you were in a highly charged emotional state when the event occurred. For example, let's assume you felt relatively neutral about heights. One day, you went hiking with a friend and slipped. You were on the edge of a cliff, gripping the wall of a canyon with all your might. You looked down. Sheer terror shot through your stomach like an arrow. Your companion dropped to the ground, leaned over the crevice, and grabbed you. You struggled back up to solid ground. From that moment forward, you had an intensely reinforced program called fear of heights.

In general, excluding highly charged emotionally intense events, momentum is developed by doing something over and over and over again. When you learned to tie your shoes, your parents guided your hands through the process. One day, you were fairly proficient at tying your shoes. Now, when you put on a pair of shoes, you automatically tie them. You do it when your mind is focused on something else.

When you are consciously trying to reprogram your subconscious mind by adding a new habit, you want to develop momentum. Generally, the more time you have invested, the more momentum you have. When we break momentum, we are breaking habits. If you break habits for any length of time, you have to form them again. If you have been doing something regularly and stop, you have to reeducate yourself. A person exercises regularly for years, takes a nasty spill while biking, and breaks a leg. This person breaks the exercise habit for three months while in a cast. When the cast comes off, the rehabilitation cycle is painful. The momentum toward exercise has been broken. Energy for exercise is now at rest. It will take a conscious, focused, persistent effort toward developing exercise enthusiasm and momentum again. The cast confined the leg and the momentum. It is not as though one can just pick up where one left off. One can build up over time, but the momentum has to rebuild.

When momentum is applied to a well-formed habit you are trying to modify or a new project you are trying to develop—and you shift priorities away from it for a while—you are likely to take up your recovery time with something new. On some level, it seems easier to get interested in something else than to go back to that project—even when the time is available. People who diet throughout their lives are more likely to try a new method each time than to go back to a technique they previously used, even if it was successful. Momentum, once broken, is difficult to regain. (Action Guide 26)

It is important to be cognizant of the relationship of flow to momentum. The effectiveness that surrounds regular activities begins to lag when you address them infrequently. If one regularly devotes one hour per day to an effort, that is effective. One hour per week is much less effective. With five hours every two weeks, the flow is interrupted and your timing will be off. That is why it is important to choose activities in alignment with your goals and priorities—something you are willing to deal with on a regular basis and are excited about. Use momentum to your advantage. Energy in motion tends to remain in motion.

In chapter 6, we will be dealing with how to set up your calendar to allocate events in your life for the most effectiveness. We will conceptually look at time from the standpoint of specific and generic time. Specific time relates to orchestration of your annual calendar to reflect the overall composition of your year (days working, days off, continuing education, vacation, and specific family days). You are going to plan your year so you will have the opportunity to carve out regular time for all major events that will comprise your year. Generic time relates to the details of the composition of each day. For example, rise at 5:00, meditate until 5:30, exercise until 6:00, work from 8:00–6:00, have family time from 7:00–9:00, and review the day until 10:00. Generic schedules can be different on weekends, and they are modified around specific schedules. People who travel a lot, especially for business, have a lot more challenges in designing consistent schedules. The better you can manage your generic schedule to remain consistent no matter where you are, the better you will take care of yourself. The amount of sleep you get, your exercise, and the foods you eat will remain in alignment.

When you are attempting to add a new habit or shift a non-resourceful habit, you want to set up as many reinforcements in your universe as you can. Creating a schedule that includes regular time to deal with this focused area is a positive tool to establish and routinely incorporate this new activity. It is a way to help you work the plan once you have established the plan. Not establishing a designated block of time on a regular basis to work on this new habit is very much like trying to save money after everything else has been paid. There is never anything left over. Effective people learned that you have to pay yourself first in order to save money. If you want to direct your time and energy in a new direction, you must block out the time to do it. If you are already a busy person, you will likely never have a free block of time. You have to create the time in your schedule first. Once you have had the courage to do this, it is amazing how you will consciously and unconsciously find the time by changing your pace or reducing your attention to some of the time robbers. You can buy back some time or reprioritize some of your activities. When you are committed and take a stand, it is as though Providence moves in to assist you.

We have talked about persistence on a number of occasions, and this concept is important when applied with a sense of urgency. The majority of people are ready to throw their aims and purposes overboard and give up at the first sign of opposition or misfortune. A few carry on despite all opposition until they attain their goals. Henry Ford, Thomas Edison, Mother Teresa, and Madame Curie were producers.

Lack of persistence is one of the major causes of failure, and it is a weakness common to the majority of "almosts". The producers seem to enjoy insurance against failure. Sometimes it appears as a hidden guide—Universal Intelligence, Spirit, God—whose duty it is to test us in all sorts of discouraging experiences. Those who pick themselves up after defeats and keep on trying arrive.

The hidden guide lets no one enjoy great achievement without passing the persistence test. Those who can take it are bountifully rewarded for their persistence. They receive, as their compensation, whatever goal they are pursuing, and they receive something infinitely more important than material compensation or the object of their quest. In *Think and Grow Rich* Napoleon Hill said, "They understand that every failure brings with it the seed of an equivalent advantage. They do not accept defeat as anything more than a temporary setback."

Four simple steps lead to the habit of persistence.

1. A definite purpose, backed by a burning desire for its fulfillment.
2. A definite plan, expressed in continuous action.
3. A mind closed tightly against all negative and discouraging influences, including negative suggestions of relatives, colleagues, and friends.
4. A friendly alliance with one or more people who will encourage one to follow through with both plan and purpose (a mastermind group).

Persistence changes a person's character as carbon changes brittle iron into invincible steel. When the going gets tough, you'll see how the tough get going.

To use a sense of urgency to its best advantage, you must stay conscious in your interactions. With time abundance, consciousness is your frame of reference. Set goals and establish priorities in alignment with your core values. Focus your behavior on goal-achieving activities, and with persistence of focus and action, you gain momentum. Persist, persist, persist. If the first plan you adopt does not work, replace it with a new plan. If this new plan fails to work, replace it with another—and another--- until you find a plan that works.

Humans are not random creatures. We do everything we do for a reason. There is a driving force behind everything we do. Every habit we have and every action we take is motivated by the need to avoid pain or gain pleasure. Most of us will exert more effort to avoid pain than to gain pleasure. For most people, the fear of loss is far greater than the desire to gain.

Let's say you have saved $200,000. Most of us would go to far greater effort to secure the $200,000 already acquired than to create another $200,000. This is avoiding the pain of loss rather than gaining the pleasure of more. Many people put in far more hours at work out of fear of losing their positions than driving themselves to advance their careers, their love of work, or helping the people they serve. In personal relationships, people spend time with family they do not especially enjoy to avoid the complaints and criticism that they are never around.

The gift of closer, warmer connections and the opportunity to create better foundations of relationships are less motivating than the need to avoid hassles. Unless you create positive goals, you will find that much of your action is a response to a judgment you have made about a current result you do not like. For many people, life is a reaction against, rather than movement toward, a conscious choice. Why do you suppose people consistently experience pain and fail to move toward something more positive? They have not reached *emotional threshold*. Emotional threshold happens when you hit a level of pain for which you are no longer willing to settle. This is the magical point when pain becomes your friend. Emotional threshold will drive you to take new actions to produce new results—even if the action you take leads to a more positive result.

Your consciousness comes from scarcity. Your goal was to avoid pain. Once you have taken action and improved things a bit, you will often backslide once you are more comfortable. Your life becomes a seesaw of events. It is like there is a cybernetic governor (an early Greek term relating to the study of a "governing" control of our functions)—a science of choice over instinct, above which you cannot reach and below which you will not fall. Rather, it contains (limits) you within a specified range of actions/behaviors unique to each person. You can absolutely alter this specified zone of familiarity, but it will take persistent, repetitive action outside your set points of comfort to shift your ceiling limit higher on a permanent basis. Take advantage of your emotional threshold. When your pain level is at maximum, focus on all the benefits of moving toward pleasure.

One of the most stifling behaviors many of us exhibit is procrastination. It is the polar opposite of persistence. Procrastination is the habit of putting off something intentionally that should be done. Napoleon Hill said, "The habit of putting off until tomorrow that which should have been done last year."

Creating alibis and excuses is closely related to doubt, worry, the refusal to accept responsibility when it can be avoided: a lack of willingness to compromise and to use difficulties as stepping stones to advancement; bargaining with life for a penny instead of demanding prosperity, opulence, riches, contentment, and happiness; planning what to do if and when overtaken by failure instead of burning all bridges and making retreat impossible; weakness, self-doubt, expecting poverty instead of demanding riches, and association with those who accept poverty instead of seeking the company of those who demand and receive riches.

Procrastination is when you know you should do something, but you still don't do it. It can be channeled in many ways. Some people procrastinate by doing passive things like sleeping, daydreaming, watching TV, chatting on Facebook, calling friends, or reading. Procrastination can involve organizing drawers, playing extra rounds of golf, or putting a bookcase together when you don't need access to the books that have been in the box for two years. Procrastination does not necessarily appear indolent. In fact, for those of us who are always on the go, it can look busy. Being busy is not necessarily being productive or effective. When you are doing an activity and a nagging voice reminds you of something else, you would be wise to check if you need to be doing the thing you are doing more than the thing you are thinking about. Procrastination costs us psychic energy, and it can make us "almosts".

Why do people procrastinate? After all, it is a conscious decision, without an effective outcome. We procrastinate when we believe that taking action in the moment would be more painful than putting it off. There comes a time in the procrastination cycle when we feel compelled to get something done. That is the moment when we changed what we linked to pain and pleasure. Suddenly, not taking action became more painful than putting it off. Notice the motivator was the avoidance of pain.

If we link massive pain to any emotional pattern or behavior, we avoid indulging in it at all costs. We can use this understanding to our benefit by changing what we link to pain and what we link to pleasure. Imagine a person who has been on multiple diets, which is not hard to do given the plethora of diet programs, books, workshops, counseling, and support groups. The focus is on avoiding fat rather than being lean. A person who is overweight has linked pleasure with the taste of fatty foods and pain with giving them up. This person might be able to override these mental associations for a while, but as the pounds are shed, the problem only seems to have been solved since the cause has not been eliminated. Consider how a person thinks about food and exercise. When the person links pain and pleasure, the problem will resurface. Going on a diet and overriding pain in the short run by pure willpower does not last. Ultimately, in order for the change to last, we must link pain to our old behavior and pleasure to our new behavior. People who are fit and healthy believe that nothing tastes as good as being thin feels. They link pleasure to healthy foods and pain to fatty foods.

We are the only creatures on the planet who have the ability to think in the abstract. It is not our results or the events that matter to us. It is our interpretation that seals our fate. If we fail to direct our associations of pain and pleasure, we live no better than animals because we simply react to the environment. To get the results you want, link massive pleasure to the outcome and the steps to the outcome. Link massive pain to not creating your image. Get emotionally involved with your image and create lasting change. The key element here is to direct your associations to use pain and pleasure resourcefully.

You will notice the primary focus in this program is on your consciousness as the cornerstone of your behaviors. It is almost axiomatic to look at someone's behaviors and results to see what he or she is really thinking about most rather than what he or she says. In fact, our results are the physical manifestation of our most repetitive thoughts, beliefs, and fears. We get what we think about most. The majority of people live life in reverse. They behave and question why when things didn't turn out the way they wanted or expected. People are much less inclined to ask questions when things are going well. The questions begin to take on negative connotations. We ask questions to avoid pain rather than posing questions that will lead to repetitive pleasure. For example, think about how many times you hear people say, "Why does this always happen to me? Why was I so stupid?" Your brain will find an answer. If you want repetitive pleasure, ask yourself empowering, resourceful questions. "How can I modify what I just did to get a more effective outcome next time? What lessons did I learn to make me more knowledgeable and insightful? How can I use this information in the future to create more positive outcomes?" Your brain will answer the questions posed to it. Get in the habit of asking better questions. It is an excellent idea to ask empowering questions, and it is even more effective to ask them prior to taking action.

When one is focused on time-abundance consciousness and truly believes, he or she will complete the necessary things that are defined as important. Spend time doing things of value that take you closer to your goals. The behaviors that follow are naturally more effective. Procrastination is an omnipresent behavior. From a consciousness perspective, the goal should be to identify the pattern at the outset and link massive pain with continuing the procrastination cycle and massive pleasure with completing the tasks one has been inclined to avoid.

There are practical solutions to task management that will help you move yourself along. The problem is often in thinking of the project as one huge, overwhelming task. Multiple tasks seem to fuse into one amorphous mountain in your mind so you feel helpless. This can happen easily in our information society. The volume of mail that comes across your desk at work and across your threshold at home on a daily basis is awesome. If you take a vacation, upon your return, it seems the dump truck has left its entire load for you.

The new material does not stop while you are clearing up the backlog. To be effective, you must find ways to deal with information as we transfer from a paper to a paperless society. What happened to that promise thirty years ago? We are barreling ahead in the information society.

Many of us manage the retrieval and management of information in different ways. Those who grew up without computers perhaps have the greatest challenge. Some still do things the old-fashioned way with paper, and some have one foot in each threshold, partially working with paper and trying to become computer literate. Younger generations use computers like those raised in bilingual households. Computers are innately a second language; you will benefit from some basic techniques to help overcome procrastination.

Practical Solution 1: Do the Worst First

Try to set things up so you first handle the project or group of projects you most resist. Whether it is making an uncomfortable telephone call or tackling a big pile of paperwork, get it done first. The energy you will feel can be used more effectively in other areas of your life.

Practical Solution 2: Divide and Conquer

Break big tasks into smaller parts and commit to doing a portion each day.

Practical Solution 3: Create Time Blocks

Sometimes we put things off because we need chunks of time to do it, and a typical day does not have free time. Use off-center time for the desired task. Get up one hour earlier every morning and commit to using that time only for the specified project.

Practical Solution 4: Circle in Toward Completion

Handle a big job in rounds, moving in from the broader generalities to the specifics. When you get down to each specific page, handle it the first time you pick it up.

Practical Solution 5: Start Anywhere

When you feel overwhelmed, be arbitrary. Start anywhere. Once started, if you find you could be more effective by restructuring, at least you're on your way.

Practical Solution 6: Planning Action

Some projects are so big that starting anywhere has you running in circles without direction, and you cannot see how to break down the project into manageable parts. The best way to handle this type of procrastination is to stop completely and identify the action elements necessary to complete the project. Write down every element that comes to mind. Do not worry about getting things into proper order or sequence. Just get them down on paper. After identifying some of the actions, you will find some obviously precede others. This is the process I went through in developing this program. As I began to develop the larger program, the complexity, variety, and volume of information seemed unwieldy at times. They were very much related and needed to be integrated. I put together a mini-program of the larger program and called it "Time Compass." The time-liberation action guide is the product of that program. The guide to assessing time in life became my blueprint.

You have now completed the lesson on sense of urgency. Begin to link massive pleasure with developing a refined sense of urgency, and link massive pain with procrastination. You may wish to review the questions and your responses in the action guide before reading the next chapter.

Chapter 4

YOUR PARADIGM SHIFT

Close your eyes for a moment and get in touch with the emotions they elicit.

- Sounds of gunshots and voices of men screaming on a battlefield with "Dixie" playing in the background.
- Think of the Gettysburg Address or "Mine Eyes Have Seen the Glory."
- Think of Martin Luther King's "I Have a Dream."

A paradigm shift for the whole nation began with the vision of Abraham Lincoln. In 1863, he was able to articulate that a nation of democracy includes all of her people. He looked at the similarities of the people rather than the differences that alienated them, and he took a powerful stand for change. That shift has been reinforced in the United States through legislation, social action, and courageous acts. It continues today, more than a hundred years later. Energy and repetition are required to initiate and sustain the shift until the shift is habitual.

Hello again. This is Dr. Hildebrand, and I want to welcome you to Chapter 4, and important one in the on time program.

In a societal context, we talk about perceiving lack of time and time pressure all the time. Time is perceived to have taken on so much control over our lives that many of us have stopped making choices about time. In fact, many of us fail to realize we have choices about how we deal with time. An article in the *Wall Street Journal* typifies the emotional stranglehold many people feel about time. For one week, the reporter followed a highly successful architect who described time as her mortal enemy. This professional's work schedule early in her career was one hundred hours per week. She pared it down to seventy or eighty hours per week.

We have choices, but as long as we do not perceive and take responsibility for our use of time, we are victims. We can choose to take charge of time in our lives. It is a must for quality of life, health, relationships, and success.

People wait for circumstances and conditions to dictate how they will reserve and spend their time. They fail to treat time like the precious resource it is. Plan, reserve, and use it for things you value most. There is a simple secret. If you are ready to take charge of time, just do it.

A paradigm shift can be initiated outside of our own thoughts. From outside, it can be perceived as being forced upon us by circumstances. The paradigm shift related to the Swiss watch industry is a good example of this. Although the Swiss invented the digital watch technology, they were so wedded to the history of the fine Swiss movement mechanical watch that they failed to convert to digital technology. Within several years, the Japanese seized the opportunity, developed the technology that was invented by the Swiss, and captured 80 percent of the market. In that case, the paradigm shift was embraced and driven by one culture and resisted by another. It gained momentum quickly once initiated.

Paradigms exist within us individually and in groups. Identify the elements of a paradigm shift to help you initiate the changes and specific strategies to help you sustain a change. Use these techniques to reinforce a change. Initiating, sustaining, and reinforcing elements of change are important interrelated topics.

First, let us deal with initiating change. When we talk about initiating change, we deal with decisions, goals, core values, and awareness.

A paradigm shift begins with a decision. Is time a problem for you? Is your life filled with events that primarily have little meaning for you? Do the events of your life have meaning? Are you concentrating on a limited aspect of your life to the exclusion of things you value more? Make a decision today to change that. Make a decision and determine the strategy. Figure out how decisions are the father of action.

Action is the highest form of affirmation. That is because all our dreams and plans, our heart's desires, can only take place if we take action. The most powerful way to shape our lives is to take action. What determines what actions you will take? Who will you become? What is your ultimate destiny in life? They are your decisions. The past does not equal the future unless you say so. In a split second, you can change directions. Have you ever had the experience of looking at something all your friends said was hard to do? Somewhere deep inside you, you decided that it was not going to be your experience. It was going to be a piece of cake, and so as the process unfolded, Providence seemed to move in to help you at every turn. When you could have become discouraged, you refused. When the goal was reached it was an empowering journey for you.

The decisions we make change our destinies. If you do not consciously make decisions, if you abdicate your responsibility for decisions—including your decisions about time—that is already a decision. You have made a decision to let yourself be directed by the environment, conditions, and circumstances.

Using the power principle of decision gives you the capacity to overcome any excuse and change any part of your life in an instant. Decisions can change your relationships, your income, your physical fitness, and your emotional state. If you decide, you can do almost anything. If someone else has done it before you, you absolutely can do it. It is a question of finding out exactly what they do, making subtle distinctions, and modeling their behavior.

Decisions bring order to your mind. No one can see you making decisions, but they will almost always see the results of your decisions. Indecision sets up conflicting energies that destabilize your mind. Psychiatrists call this internal conflict *ambivalence.*

People who have strong decision-making capabilities have a strong self-image and high self-esteem. They possess confidence. Indecision and ambivalence are characteristic in people with low self-esteem. Decision makers are not fearful of making errors. They usually have a governing rule from which they operate. They learn from errors. They do not see an error as a failure. They believe that failing at something does not make one a failure. Only quitting makes one a failure. Winning is a decision.

Effective decisions must be backed by discipline. Highly successful people make decisions quickly and change them slowly. The most natural thing in the world is to follow the crowd. We have been conditioned to follow the crowd. Historically, the crowd often moves in the wrong direction. Get in the habit of making your own decisions. Follow your inner guide and do not be influenced by the decisions of others. His research discovered that decision makers had a number of common characteristics. They found work a pleasure and enjoyed work and play equally. These people followed their own values—not those of society, parents, or other people.

Commitment is a corollary element that goes with decisions. Most of us have weak decision-making muscles. We do not realize what it means to make a real decision. We fail to recognize the force of change that a truly congruent, committed decision makes. Part of our problem is that we use the term decision so loosely that it has come to describe our wishes, not our commitments. Instead of making decisions, we state our preferences. The word decision comes from the Latin roots, with *de* meaning down or away from and *caedere* meaning to cut. Therefore, a decision means cutting from any other possibility. A true decision means you are committed to achieving a result and cutting yourself off from any other possibility. Committed decisions show up in two places: your calendar and your checkbook. No matter what you say you value, or even think your priorities are, you have only to look at last year's calendar and checkbook to see the decisions you have made about what you truly value. For example, I am committed to growth, both professionally and personally. A review of my calendar always shows multiple continuing-education courses, seminars, and workshops in personal growth as well as in my profession. My checkbook is filled with tuition disbursements and purchases of books and videos. See how you have reserved your time. Look at your expenditures. Those are the trails to the decisions you have made.

Decision-making is hard because decisions deal with changes that count. After making a true decision, especially tough ones, we usually feel a tremendous burden has been lifted from our shoulders. Even when the decisions we have made seem to create a sacrifice or something lost in the short run, it is a relief to have a clear, unquestioned objective. The way to make better decisions is to make more of them.

How do you recognize a true decision? Action always flows from a true decision. As Mark Twain said, the secret to getting ahead is getting started. The secret to getting started is to find some mechanism to break down complex, overwhelming tasks into small, manageable tasks. Start with the first one. The six techniques to overcome procrastination discussed in chapter 3 are wonderful tools to utilize in getting started and keeping the flow toward completion moving in a timely fashion.

Decisions must be made consciously. Without making your decisions consciously, you abdicate responsibility for the outcome. Let me give you an example from my own life. For years I have carried a day-timer organizer. Whenever a professional or social presented event itself, I picked up my organizer. If there were an open slot, I would simply fill it in. In the past, I managed my calendar from open slots on a piece of paper I filled in as long as there was an opening. I never even questioned whether I wanted to do something or if the addition of the current item complemented the overall scheme of my oth er commitments. After all, I had a lot of energy. I would just make it work.

I was abdicating my responsibility with my schedule by letting everyone else's priorities supersede my own. I never checked in with myself to see whether the event met my needs or goals or if it was timed effectively with my other priorities in mind. I just made the schedule work out without paying conscious attention to how each individual entry had an effect on the whole experience of my life. Making this distinction had a powerful impact on my life. I learned that I am responsible for the condition, content, and flow of the events I schedule. If I do not attend to my schedule consciously it will be a mishmash of events.

I was busy all the time and not experiencing the levels of satisfaction and joy I wanted to be routine in my life. I solved this dilemma life by utilizing specific and generic calendars, which we will discuss in much greater depth in chapter 6. It is an exciting concept, and by structuring my events with these tools, I orchestrate my schedule and take conscious responsibility for its content. I reserve time for the things I value most. I do not leave to chance that I can squeeze in events with people I love or organizations I value.

Finally, let us talk about advance decisions. Just like we make advance bookings for dinner at a fine restaurant or an airline flight, we can eliminate a lot of problems by making decisions well in advance. When you have reached a decision to reduce your weight and get fit, it would be wise, prior to your arrival at the restaurant, to decide in advance what you will choose. Decide upon at least one of your best options. In order for your life to be filled with millions of moments that have meaning for you, a specific calendar needs to be set up in advance for the year. Reserve and set aside days or portions of days for things you value. Include work, family time, and other things to ensure that you are going to have a balanced and inclusive life.

Set aside time in advance for events and people you love. That is action flowing from your consciousness. Make it work. I met two interesting entrepreneurial gentlemen; one was Canadian, and the other was from Illinois. They each owned their own real estate agencies and made seven-figure incomes. They both had a commitment to a high degree of success, but they also had a commitment to spending time with their families. They worked hard at creating a structure in their businesses to have things run effectively. They refused to take work home on the weekends.

Many people would think they had special circumstances, but they each had a core belief and value that family time was sacrosanct. They created schedules, support teams, and structure around this core value. They made their businesses conform to their value about family relationships. Too many of us come from an emotional place of thinking we will spend quality time with our families after we get our work done. Work is like dirty laundry. It keeps coming around, particularly in our information/technology-overload society. There is almost never time when you could not be working. Nobody on a deathbed ever said, "I wish I had spent more time working." For your life to be comprised of the things you value, you must make decisions and take action from what you want—not what you think you can eke out. Advance planning can be a way to reserve the time for the variety of events you love and want to preserve in your life.

The biggest hurdle to overcome in making decisions is overcoming the fear of making the wrong decision. Let me set your mind at ease right now. You will make wrong decisions in your life. Mistakes, as they are termed, are part of the human experience. If we have an underlying value that says we learn from our mistakes, we have a winning formula.

Thomas Edison said, "I am not discouraged because every wrong attempt discarded is another step forward." He tried and failed in thousands of different experiments to create the incandescent light. Look at the result of his efforts. Every decision made out of fear is destructive. Every decision made out of love is empowering and gives you the opportunity to make better decisions later.

There are two hemispheres of your brain. The left side of the brain controls your intellect. It is the logical, methodical, mechanical part of who you are. The right side of your brain is your emotional, creative side. We all use both sides of our brain, but most of us have a dominant side. Artistic, creative, entrepreneurial people are usually right-brain dominant. Scientific, mathematical, and managerial people are usually left-brain dominant. It is an interesting phenomenon that decisions are a right-brain function. We have glorified the left-brain, logical, scientific approach in Western culture to gather data and reach our decisions. That is not the process. Decisions are not made after a lot of analysis. We make decisions and justify the decisions with data. Since we invariably try to make ourselves right, our brains will pull in all the data to support our decisions and exclude data that varies from our choices.

Let us say you have walked into a jewelry store to purchase a watch. You tell the salesman what you are looking for, and he picks up the finest watch in that category. "Let me just get an idea of size and shape. Let's try this one on."

Your brain immediately says, "I want this."

On a precognitive level, you have made the decision that you want this watch. You have made the decision emotionally, instantly, and permanently through the right hemisphere of the brain. Now you need to logically justify your decision by collecting more and more data. This is your left brain in action. You might surface some objections about it being too expensive, but most good salesmen know if they can help you find a way to fund it, even if it is far more money than you wanted to spend, you will find logical ways to justify this emotional decision.

Let us summarize some important concepts about decisions. The first step in initiating change is understanding that your destiny will be shaped by the quality of your decisions. Make committed decisions on your own, based on your own values. Make them frequently, consciously, and in advance. Do not worry about whether they will be wrong. If you have made an error, you will learn from it—and a more effective action will follow in the future. Notice that action always follows your decisions. If action does not follow, you did not make a decision—you simply toyed with the idea.

Paradigm shifts begin with confrontations with yourself. If you feel a bit uncomfortable, rejoice. You cannot break through a terror barrier until you get up close and personal with it.

We talked briefly about goal-achieving activities in chapter 3. We are going to talk more about goals, the second element in initiating change, later. It is important to be aware that goals are only a means. When you set goals in alignment with your values, you feel the richness of accomplishment. Have you ever had the experience of setting a goal, working hard to accomplish it, and wondered if that is all there is? Goals set up without consideration of your values do not really meet your needs. It is not the events or experiences themselves but the meaning we have attached to them that counts for us. Reaching goals that are not attached to core values have little meaning for us.

Have you ever found yourself in a situation in which you had a difficult time making a decision? You were not clear about what you valued most in that situation. All decision-making comes down to values clarification. When you know what is important to you, making a decision is simple. Most people are unclear about what is most important in their lives; therefore, decision-making becomes a form of internal conflict.

Each of us lives according to a unique set of core values, the third element in initiating change. These governing values are things that are most important to you. They include traits and beliefs like honesty, love, and belief in a higher power. They are fundamental elements of your personality, and you might not even be able to articulate their importance. On an essential level, they are important to you. Other governing values, like the desire for financial security or the need to make a difference, represent mega-goals that we feel driven to accomplish. Your governing values are represented by the clearest answers you can give to certain questions. What are your highest priorities? Which of these priorities do you value most?

Many people have not gone through the process of clearly defining their deepest values. They are clear about some of them, but they cannot articulate others clearly. It is difficult to live your life by a set of hazy standards. It would be like trying to get to California from the East Coast without a map. You know the general direction, but your journey will be more direct with fewer detours with a mapped-out plan.

To see whether you live your life based upon your highest priorities, you have to ask yourself a question: Is what I do on a regular basis what really matters in my life?

Even though our governing values are our highest priorities, there often exists a gap between our ideals and our present realities. Although the execution of our values is never perfect, the closer our daily activities align with our values, the more we experience what Abraham Maslow termed self-actualization. It is a merger of what you do with what you value.

To make it a bit more complex, we have certain rules of behavior to support what we value, and what makes relationships more complicated is we express our values through different rules of conduct. For example, let us take two people in a relationship who say that love is a top priority. Their rules about how to express love are very different. One person has a rule that says if you really love someone, you show it by providing a lavish lifestyle. The other person's rule is when you really love someone, you spend a lot of time telling him or her how much you care. It is possible the person who shows love by being a terrific provider is not around much because she/he is out there slaying the dragon. The person who loves to spend a lot of time talking and nurturing does not have the object of his or her affection around much because of financial strains/demands. This is a classic example of how people can talk about having a priority of value for love, but the rules for expression are entirely different.

It is helpful to know our governing values, their hierarchical priorities, and our rules for expressing them. It is also helpful to be aware that every argument, disappointment, or misunderstanding you have ever had with another person is because you have violated someone's rules—or they have violated yours.

The only reliable source of stability in this world of accelerated change and increasing ambiguity and complexity is a strong inner core and the willingness to change and adapt everything except that core. It is far more important to understand who you are than where you are going since where you are going will almost certainly change. Let's begin this process of values clarification with some of my values and the rules I have to support them. After that, develop your own list in the form of affirmations. Some of my core or governing values are:

1. I am loving.

- I accept the unique expressions of our differences as people and look for our similarities with each other and our source.
- I am gentle and understanding with myself and others.
- I express my feelings of love, appreciation, and gratitude often.
- I contribute freely and generously to every endeavor and relationship with which I am involved.

2. I seek growth.

- I open my mind and heart to experiences to extend my understanding and stretch beyond my comfort zone.
- I strive every day to enhance my knowledge toward more effective action.
- I am on a constant journey to understand more broadly, share more generously, and make a bigger difference to life in general.
- I reserve time for personal growth, relationships, and professional aspirations.
- I create balance.

3. I am prosperous.

- I set goals, move toward them regularly, and meet or exceed them.
- I am grateful for the bounty in my life of health, loving relationships, wealth, and growth.
- I am an expert in my endeavors. My actions are effective, and I receive great rewards.

- I love to work, contribute, make a difference, and graciously receive the abundance that flows from that effort.

I currently have twelve governing values ranked in hierarchical order of priority and rules to support them. Although I gave you examples of three of my governing values and rules to support them, only the first and second represent their true places in their order on my list. In fact, prosperity, which I listed as third for purposes of an example, is my sixth value.

I am certainly a work in progress. We are all on life's journey. I do not always act in alignment with my values; as I review my values, I find it helpful to imagine myself as I want to be. I imagine a finished Carole Hildebrand. When I keep this vision of the finished Carole in front of my eyes, I find it easier to do the things that will help me be the person I want to be.

Are governing values cast in stone? Can we ever change them? Absolutely. Governing values are like the Constitution. Over time, as you grow and change, there are elements you want to add or emphasize. The hierarchical order and content of your values list can shift. Certain values will likely be a part of every values list you create. Some will change.

As you reposition the order of your list, you will notice the time you reserve and allocate for various events in your life can dramatically change. One of my twelve values is being healthy and fit. On the physical level, I do not drink or smoke. I am not diligent about eating only foods that support health, and if my daily calendar is filled, and a new event is introduced, I will almost invariably give up exercising as my first step in reorganizing my schedule rather than extending a deadline on something else that needs to be done that day. You might say not drinking and not smoking are absolute musts in my life, but exercising is still too frequently a "should".

I have times when I am maximally focused on all the aspects of the elements necessary to support my value to health and fitness, and I make choices to honor that fully. When the heat gets high enough and something needs to be reprioritized, exercise is the first thing I allow myself to slide on. Which of the things you say you value will you slide on?

Compile your own list of values and rules of behavior to support those values. This process can take time, but reserve the time to do it effectively. These are your values. They are the heart of who you are. To structure a life in alignment with your values, you need to know precisely what your current ones are. Give yourself the gift of the time to get the job done. Using my values as an example, list twenty qualities in the form of affirmations that are most important to you. They do not yet need to be in any particular order. Just list what is most important to you. Rank the order of priority of these values and then condense your broader list of twenty down to your biggest, most important values. For some, you might condense a lot. For others, you might reduce your list only slightly. These values define you. Of the twenty, what qualities define you?

List your rules of behavior to support your values. To help you define how you will express your values, it is helpful to determine what has to happen for you to feel blank. The blank is the word or words you choose to describe your value.

On my list, my number one value is: "I am loving." When I am being loving, I accept the unique expressions of our differences as people and look for our similarities with each other and our connectedness to the God energy, the source. When I am being loving, I am gentle and understanding with myself and others. When I am being loving, I express my feelings of loving, appreciation, and gratitude often.

Define your own rules of behavior. Do you have a deeper understanding of who you are? What do you value? Do your rules of behavior support those values? As we look at shifting paradigms, we will be involved with decisions, values, rules, goals, and priorities. How do we make the changes last?

For changes to be of true value, they must be consistent and lasting. We have all had the experience of reaching emotional threshold and making a decision that we must change. With full emotional intensity, we move forward in alignment with the change. When we meet resistance, we persist. When we meet more resistance, we persist. Whether it is a personal habit or the habit of a family, a company, a country, or the world, if the habit we are trying to change is deeply ingrained, it will take incredible persistence and momentum to overcome the current paradigm. After all, the current paradigm got strong because it was supported by repetition over time. It could be centuries of reinforcement. The resistance to change is powerful. Getting started is the first step, but you have to be concerned with how to sustain the change.

With a broader sphere of change, you are either part of the resistance or part of the momentum to change. Global change takes place one person at a time, and as momentum builds, more people add their energy. Mass and motion together equal speed. That is how huge paradigm shifts work. For purposes of our discussion, we are going to talk about individual change, but the principles are the same.

For a person to create lasting change, there are essentially three steps. First, you must raise your standards. Second, you must change your limiting beliefs. And third, you must change your strategy.

In order to raise your standards, you must change what you demand of yourself absolutely, consistently, and persistently. You must look at the things you aspire to become, and you must identify those things you will no longer accept in your life. Decide you will tolerate no less than acting in alignment with your core values.

Without taking charge of your belief systems, you can raise your standards to the sky, but you will never have the conviction to back them up. You must change your limiting beliefs. Your limiting beliefs are reverse values. They represent your worst fears. In chapter 3, we said you will do more to avoid pain than you will to gain pleasure. It takes genuine commitment to remain conscious and focused on what you want. The pull to unconscious, passively ingested information is strong. And much of this information directs you to focus on what is not working. Fear-based information is responsible for your limiting beliefs. There must be congruence or harmony between your beliefs and actions for lasting change to occur. You must alter your limiting beliefs. (Explore your attitude toward change in Action Guide)

The third step to lasting change is changing your strategy. To enable your commitment to change anything, you must have a good strategy. One of the best strategies around is modeling. Find someone who is outstanding at doing something you want to be able to do. Learn what they do, their core beliefs, how they think, and how they and act. Do what they do, and you will create similar results. Refine what they do, and you will get even better results. The secret is in the action. You must take action. Based on results, a lot of people know—but few people do. The people who consistently do are the producers. They contribute the most, and they receive the lion's share of the world's rewards.

What is the purpose of life? Can you accept a simple statement? Can you grow and expand? Can you grow in connectedness to your spirituality, your relationships, and your physical body? Nature grows by a patterned plan, but we have choices. We choose how we grow in understanding and when we grow. We choose the rate at which we grow. The more distinctions we can make about any aspect of humans on this three-dimensional plane relative to our relationships to the life force from which we emanate, the more of life we are experiencing. There is no end to growth. One of the most basic, dynamic laws of life is creating or disintegrating. All energy is in constant motion. Toward expansion or constriction. Toward more or less. Up or down. Energy does not stay still. The nucleus of your being is spirit, and it is always for growth. It is never for disintegration.

Awareness and understanding give meaning to life. Awareness is like shining a light on the darkness so you can see. The more you focus on any aspect of life, the more evident it will become to you. The more you focus on financial success, the more elements of that game will become evident to you. It will have a context to your culture and era and your talents and resources. There will be natural laws with which your thoughts and behaviors must harmonize.

As you focus in greater detail on the subtle distinctions of success, you will inevitably go in search of a greater body of understanding. It is like standing on a riverbank with a stone in your hand. As you drop the stone into the water, the water seems to surround it. The stone floats down through it, but the water on the surface has small ripples that spread out from the initial impact. The stone acts on the water, and the water acts on the stone. As you go out in search of more understanding about anything—where you are both the student and the teacher at once—every distinction you make adds to the body of knowledge of the whole.

As the person you are, you have certain themes in your life with which you will deal. You have certain awareness and understandings toward which you gravitate. Disconnected distinctions have limited impact, and orderly growth has full impact. In an infinite sense, everything is connected. In order to function effectively in our finite world, we deal with the levels of diverse information with some degree of structure. We want enough structure to help us organize information and deal with it—but not so much structure that we eliminate creativity.

Set goals in alignment with what you value. Your life themes will provide you with the structure to grow. Expand your awareness in an orderly and effective way. You are a perfect expression of an infinite power. As you become more consciously aware of your oneness with the infinite power within you, as well as its laws of expression, that awareness will be reflected in your outcomes.

To understand goals a little better, let us talk about what they are. You hear people say that their only goals in life are happiness and peace of mind. Some people mistake happiness and peace of mind for goals. They are not goals. Happiness and peace of mind are conditions of life that all thinking people want, but they are not goals. They are the result of a higher degree of awareness, which are a result of doing what you need to do to achieve your goals.

The most productive people are the happiest because they are serving others. When you are giving the best you have to give, you have an emotional feeling of being filled, joyful, and happy. Peace of mind is the psychic income you receive in exchange for your effort. Awareness is the only thing that can provide happiness. Setting goals and taking aligned actions produces results. The lessons in the journey toward the goal expand awareness. It is the illumination process. Expanded awareness generates feelings of happiness and peace of mind. The goals give you direction for your efforts.

Producers set goals. Life's victors, the producers, represent only 3 percent of the population. Without exception, they believe in the concept of setting goals. It is a creative positive process. The 97 percent of the population, the "almosts", wish positively but think negatively. They fail to set goals regularly, and they do not have focused energy toward a desired destination. They look at their current results and fail to dream beyond them. By looking only at your current results, you see only your weakness. If you spend the majority of your time focusing and thinking about what is not working, you become a self-fulfilling prophecy.

If you want to win big in life, you must learn to structure your expenditure of energy through setting goals. Goals are absolutely essential, and to reach the goals we desire, we have to change. Goals will give you a direction in which to head. In the journey, you must learn to be flexible and versatile. Constantly try new things. It will not necessarily be comfortable, and your old paradigm is likely pulling you toward a familiar comfort zone.

Be willing to take risks. Thoughtful, purposeful risk-taking is a part of the creative process. I am not talking about foolish, irresponsible, thrill-seeking risk-taking. I am talking about trusting yourself as an expression of the infinite source. Be willing to head toward a future that exists only in your imagination. Set your goals way beyond where you are today. Head, with trust in yourself, toward your envisioned future.

Once you reach a committed decision in harmony with a core value to create a bigger future, you will be challenged by a lot of negative energy to keep you where you are. These negative energies are devious. They attack us from the outside while draining the life force from within. Outside of us, the power is called our environment. Inside of us, this power is referred to as negative conditioning. The subconscious mind will play mental games in an attempt to keep us locked into destructive habits.

Goals are the lighthouse toward which we head through the fog of our old paradigms. One of the particular challenges we face today is that we are bombarded by stimuli. It is difficult to know where to focus next. This makes goals even more vital than ever before. Outside stimuli are seductive. A ringing telephone, a pile of mail, a television ad, a stack of faxes, and your open computer screen vie for your attention at every turn. We need access to all of these vehicles to function in the modern world, but how do we use them without being distracted and consumed by them?

When people are overexposed to stimuli, they feel a diminished sense of self-worth and self-esteem. Even people who set goals frequently feel overwhelmed. What has not been discussed very much is the impact that too much information has on one's sense of adequacy. More and more people feel as though they are supposed to be able to handle all the information. Part of handling it is learning what is important to focus on and what you must dismiss without much inquiry. Reserve time for the things you value most; that will take you closer to your dream. We have to become experts at sorting and sifting so that we do not give energy to things that do not have meaning for us. Focusing on goals can help you set priorities. You cannot deal with all of it. Develop strategies to help you access the part of it you need to fulfill your goals.

Why do the majority of us lead such limited lives, especially in the face of so many more options? We never investigate our potential and incorrectly assume that what we have done in the past and are doing today is all we can do. We accept self-limitation. If we make changes, they are calculated and painstakingly slow. We hardly recognize them as change. To be successful in replacing negative habits, we must have goals.

Whenever you have been successful in improving habits, you have consciously or unconsciously set a goal. You found reason to do what had to be done. The greater the desire to reach the goal, the easier it is to change your conditioning.

Just as there are levels of understanding, there are levels of goals. There are things to which you aspire and things you want to acquire. The driving theme of your aspirations is your goal. It should be something you want—and not something you need. It should be something that inspires you. Only you can decide what that goal will be.

The road to your goal will be filled with many challenges. It is essential to be emotionally involved with the idea of reaching your goal. What do you want? Do not let your present situation influence your thinking or decisions.

Set a goal of achieving something so big and exhilarating that it excites and scares you at the same time. This goal must be in harmony with your core values. It will dominate your thinking. Set a goal for which you will willingly spend your time.

If you set anemic goals, your results will be lackluster. Don't set goals that are disconnected from your core/governing values. They are expressions of shoulds—not wants—and even if you achieve them, there will be no joy for you. If you focus on the past, you will get the same old thing. Set goals based on the future and new ideas.

What do you want? Some of us know immediately and can articulate it well. Others might feel shy or reserved about expressing it. Some are not quite sure or it is not a conscious thought yet. You know some things you want, but you cannot articulate the big one. Relax. Continue this program. Do the exercises with full attention, energy, and trust. Answers will percolate to the surface. In a few moments, we will go through a process to identify your goals and to determine your main goal in life, where you will focus your time.

Two other powerful concepts are related to our goals in a very essential way. They are the concepts of asking resourceful questions and transformational vocabulary. On the road to achieving your goals, you will face with many obstacles, opportunities to learn new lessons, and distinctions. You can move through those challenges with maximal growth in minimal time if you stay in a conscious, resourceful state. These two tools are available to all of us and can change the quality of our experiences. They cost nothing except your conscious attention, and when integrated into your style of conversation, you will reap powerful dividends.

Do you suppose you would come up with a different set of solutions to your time pressures if you asked more questions? How do I create time freedom in my life? How can I find a way to work less and have more time with the people I love? How can I be of more service to more people. How can I earn more money at the same time? The answers to those questions will be quite different from other questions. What technique do I need to learn to stop wasting so much time? How come, no matter how hard I work, I never have time to do the things I love?

Your mind answers every question you pose to it. Get in the habit of asking resourceful questions. If you notice yourself asking disempowering questions, shift and reframe your questions. Why am I so dumb? That question is demeaning and reinforces a negative downward energy spiral. It is hard to create energetic options from that emotional place. To reach goals, create new solutions more effectively. We want to be in a resourceful state. Asking resourceful, powerful questions over and over again will create a focus toward creative solutions.

Language is a powerful tool. When you feel confused, use the opportunity to change your choice of words to describe that emotion. The words we choose shape our emotions. Use empowering, resourceful words. Creative energy will flow more freely, and solution/manifestation will happen sooner. When you feel confused––switch your mind and your words. *I am intrigued.*

The words we use create emotions and vibrations inside our bodies. Feeling confused can have an element of loss or frustration. Feeling intrigued switches that vibration to a resourceful, inquisitive state. The process of using words to help you stay in a resourceful state is called *transformational vocabulary.* Words shape our beliefs and impact our actions. Words are the fabric from which all questions are cut.

Another way to use transformational vocabulary is to lessen the intensity of the words you use to lower the impact of negativity. If something has happened that could upset you, you can say you are furious, angry, or a little peeved. Notice the difference in your vibrations with each of these descriptions of the same event.

Use the concepts of transformational vocabulary and ask resourceful questions in your life. They will be particularly helpful in relationship to setting goals. Used effectively, these concepts will raise your energy and elevate the quality and speed of the manifestation of your results.

Human beings are naturally goal-seeking organisms. All of life is based upon the principle of creating or disintegrating. You are either improving the quality of your life or taking away from it. The choice is yours. Humans operate by choice. Take responsibility for your choices, including the way you think and behave about time. If time is a problem for you, if it is filled with far too many low-priority, low-value events, be sure your goals are in alignment with your values. Structure your focus and time allocation for events and relationships you most value.

When you were an infant, you had goals and attracted whatever assistance you required to achieve those goals. Growth and change were the order of the day from the moment you drew your first breath. When you ate, crawled, walked, and ran, you were achieving goals. They were more spontaneous goals than the thoughtful ones you began to create as your mind developed to the point that you could create abstract thoughts. The ability to work with abstract thoughts gives us the ability to generate something on the visible level from the unstructured, invisible supply.

What do you want? How do you choose a goal? The answer is simple. Dream. Take the lid off your marvelous mind and dream. Let your creative imagination go. In chapter 9, we will deal in greater detail with the process of manifestation, but it begins with a dream or an image of something you want. It is not what someone else says you should want; it is something you truly and deeply want. Do what you need to do to achieve your goals. Learn your lessons as you progress, and you will invariably be of service to others.

Prosperity is the manifestation of big, exciting, service-oriented goals. There is no virtue in poverty and no sin in wealth. In fact, poverty consciousness in thought and behavior gets more of the same. Abundance consciousness creates the right seed for the manifestation of all good things. We talked a great deal in chapters 1 and 2 about abundance consciousness as it relates to time freedom. Poverty is manifested in many ways. Feeling pressed for time, hectic, and frantic about time is poverty consciousness in action. What is more valuable on the three-dimensional level than time?

The purpose of setting goals is not to acquire things. It is to raise consciousness. The acquisition of materialistic things can provide the resources and time freedom for service to others and growth for yourself. Things provide comfort. The more comfortable you are, the more creative you can become. Then you will not be required to use your precious time or marvelous mental faculties to seek out the basic requirements necessary to survive. This will free you to create and execute big, magnificent ideas to benefit yourself—as well as many other people whose lives you touch.

Prerequisites of setting goals are imaging and wanting what you want. In other words, dreaming. Everything you see and enjoy today—the car you drive, the sofa in your living room, the computer on your desk—started out as a dream in someone's imagination.

If you are still too uncomfortable to articulate your big goal—or you still are not consciously aware—approach it sequentially. Think about anything you want. Picture it in your mind. Do not worry about how or why. Just see it and want it. See yourself on the screen of your mind already in possession of this goal. Stretch your imagination a bit. If you are already consciously aware of how to get what you want, it should not be a goal. Set goals to increase understanding. If you already know how to reach your goal, there is no risk and little growth for you. Since you likely will reach your goal but not expand your awareness, it is not a worthy goal. The purpose of a goal is to act as an incentive to make the necessary changes in your paradigm. Conditioning habits helps you reach your goals.

Many people take few risks by setting goals they know they can achieve. Make sure your goals are really exciting and interesting enough to fuel your emotions. Make your goals so big that even if you experience a failure, you are able to see it as a temporary setback—and not the end of your desire to achieve it. Do not set your goals on logic. Setting goals is about dreaming. Logic is terrific when you are solving problems, but setting goals has nothing to do with it.

Your goals come from your creative faculties, which are also called the six intellectual factors:

- reason
- will
- perception
- memory
- imagination
- intuition

Logic comes through the five senses. Your success and happiness in life is up to you. Begin the process of defining your goals—and the big goal—by creating a wants list. Go to the time-liberation action guide and list thirty things you really want. Let your imagination soar. You might want to create a huge business, travel to exotic places, study with the great minds of our times, find an enriching, loving relationship, have a big family, or spend more quality time with people you love. The sky is the limit.

You are in dreaming mode. Before you write down what you want, review your list of values. As you set your mind to dreaming, be aware of what you said you valued in the previous exercises. Your values will give focus to your wants.

Take all the time you need to complete your wants list. You might complete them in an hour. It might take you several days or a week. Give yourself the gift of doing this to completion. Dig inside yourself for answers. If you knew it was impossible to fail, what would you choose? List your thirty wants. The list does not need to be categorized or in any particular order.

If you think you do not have thirty wants, be aware that they may present themselves to you in the upcoming hours or days. Once that is done, prioritize your goals. Be aware that setting goals requires serious thought.

Zig Ziglar was a giant in the motivational/success coaching business. He said, "A goal that is casually set and lightly taken is freely abandoned at the first obstacle." If you felt challenges while creating your list, this part of the process may be challenging as well. Do it anyway. The time you invest will be richly rewarded.

The first step in prioritizing your goals is to review your list several times to become really familiar with it. Group the thirty wants into three categories and label them a, b, and c. Your a goals are the ten most important wants. Your b goals are the next ten goals. The final ten wants are your c goals, which are the least important.

Rank your goals from 1 to 10 with 1 being your top priority and 10 being the least. Do the same for categories b and c.

Rewrite your a list with your top priority goal (a-1) being the one upon which you will focus most of your conscious attention. Write your goal on your goal card in the present tense as though you are already receiving it. Carry your goal card with you everywhere, preferably in your pocket so you can touch and read it often. The process of touching it will trigger—through neuro-associations—the thought and image of your a-1 goal. If you cannot carry it in a pocket, put it in your organizer or purse. See it and touch it frequently throughout the day.

Most of your other goals will come to you as you move toward your a-1 goal. The other twenty-nine goals will be your stepping-stones.

In chapter 5, we will be talking about developing plans and setting priorities to achieve your goals. You must take massive action daily toward your goal. The pull toward old, familiar habits or resistance to change is constant. Action plans are essential for breathing life into goals. To change habits, you must have a plan that you reinforce with great regularity.

Never change your goal. Change the timetable or alter the plan, but continue to focus on the goal until it is manifested.

When you have chosen your a-1 goal, write the date by which you will have achieved this goal. If you have to extend the date, that is a simple thing to do. Transfer the information to your pocket-sized goal card enclosed in your package and carry it with you. Review it frequently throughout each day. It will bring focus and a sense of purpose to your daily activities. It will keep you in a more resourceful state. By resonating to a positive, more expansive future, your body vibration is on a higher-energy frequency. With this higher energy, you will easily and naturally deflect the downward, negative, disempowering energy as it propels toward you each day. In fact, when you are going through heightened challenges, you will want to touch and review the goal card more frequently to counterbalance the lower energy of negativity.

In this chapter, we have focused on core values and global life goals. These are visionary goals, and their fulfillment requires you to expand your awareness and understanding to achieve them. They include your big goal, and the wide group of subset goals in support of your big vision. In a sense, these two are visionary-energy goals. Task-type goals affect the orderly progression of work. We will deal with those in chapters 6 and 7 when we discuss time leveraging.

The root cause of our time problems is the way we think and behave about time. We dealt with our consciousness about time in great detail in an earlier chapter. In this segment, we have discussed the necessary elements of changing old behaviors. We want to relate the general principles of paradigm shifting to time and how you think about time. What would you like to change?

To give you the proper perspective, take a moment to review. To change any paradigm, habit, or old conditioning, it must start with a conscious, committed decision that is based upon your identified wants and core values. A decision is your line in the sand—a place from which you will not retreat. We talked in detail about your core values and your rules of behavior, which identify the actions that represent your interpretation of how you express those values. You identified your core values and rules of behavior. We talked about setting goals as a structuring technique to focus your creative energy toward a future filled with outcomes based on vision and wants rather than needs. You have identified your big goal and all the subset visionary goals to support that big goal.

Developing a new habit is not easy. Developing a group of new habits around a key theme of change is even more challenging. Refer back to review the process of change. Remember the concept of the terror barrier? In your evolution to the new paradigm, you will cross your terror barrier again and again. The more regularly you confront your discomforts about change, the easier it will become. The way to help yourself progress toward the new you is to think the thoughts you would have to think to be the new you. Think them constantly. Speak the words that harmonize with the new you. Ask empowering questions that keep you focused and think about how the new you will handle things. Everyday, in every way, think, talk, and be the new you. Set up strategies to support the new you. Tell someone you trust about something you are trying to change. Let them coach you and remind you when you are not speaking and being the new you. You will get back on track quickly. Associate with people who have values like the new you.

Decide in advance how you will reward the new you at every step along the way. Because momentum works the way it does, it takes more energy to initiate the first movement than it takes to sustain it. Give yourself plenty of positive incentives and reinforcements during your journey.

There is a wonderful rewards game to play with yourself in which you assign values to certain behaviors. You can assign rewards in fives, tens, fifties, and hundreds. A hundred-level reward might be something extraordinary like a trip to Europe. A five would be an evening at the movies, a bicycle ride, or a dinner out in the neighborhood. Obviously, rewards have to be something that sing to your heart. A bicycle ride could be heaven for one person and real work for another. Your rewards are related to wants—not shoulds. Develop a list of five-level rewards, ten-level rewards, fifty- level rewards, and hundred level rewards.

It is likely you will have a far greater variety of five-level and ten-level rewards than hundred-level rewards. If you bring work home every night, the emotional distinction between work and home is obscured. If you feel trapped, your family feels resentful, but the work still has to be handled—and you really love family time.

To handle this tug-of-war, pick two nights a week to stay one to two hours after work to get all your paperwork done. You will have three nights per week with your family. For each evening you stay later at the office, you get a ten-level reward.

If you are frequently late for work by five or ten minutes, you are probably embarrassed. You may have reprimanded yourself a million times, but you still keep doing it. Intellectually, you understand the power of being on time. Studies show that highly effective people are virtually always on time-—no excuses. Every day you are on time, give yourself something from your five-level list as your reward. Be sure to choose things you will really look forward to.

This segment has been a particularly demanding one. Changing habits takes vision, commitment, persistence, and tenacity. To get there from here, you need to understand where you are and what meaning you have placed on your behaviors. Having done the exercises, you now know your values, rules, and goals.

Does your expenditure of time reflect your values and goals? Does your expenditure of money reflect your values and goals? Review your time expenditure with various relationships and activities in a week and briefly look over your calendar and checkbooks again. Plan your perfect work and leisure days.

Congratulations. You have taken a giant step toward changing how you spend your time. Fill your moments with things and people you value and direct them toward a goal that inspires you.

Chapter 5

SETTING PRIORITIES

Your awareness of the relationship of your activities to the outcomes you desire is critical. People say they want a lot of things, but if you look at their daily behaviors, they often do not complement their dreams. You can't get there from here.

Time Continuum and Pivotal Events

Midpoint Transitioning The Rest of
Life Begins———————————--------X-----------------------------Your Time

Life Begins and the first few years are spent finding yourself, learning to relate to family, friends, exploring what you like and dislike. Then there is a transitioning Midpoint period when you begin to use what you have learned, reaching further, trying make it pay, both financially and personally. You are required to take risks, make changes in who you thought you were, make plans for the rest of your life, which requires you to focus on your behavior, sorting out the differences in your effective and ineffective behavior, setting priorities.

It becomes crucial at this stage to focus on the benefits of proper planning---for the Rest of Your Life.

The differences that present themselves to us in each generation / phase of life offer both positive and negative influences that must be sorted out by each of us as we find our way to who we are and what we want from life, what our values will look like in the later years of our lives.

This concept of Generational differences was developed by Linda Chandler, the Founder and Lead Instructor of the Core Value Training Program, which teaches ethics and principles for both personal and business life. Check out her amazing training courses. She says that companies in the new millennium will look different from companies in the 1980s. Diversity is primary. Key teams should include not only diversity of nationalities and gender, but of generations. Particularly in business, she says, it will be ideal to get all generations on your team for the most complete and effective feedback, which will help you set company priorities.

Chandler created terms that could be applied to various ages / generations, and the advantages that each could offer in a work environment:

Those 53 and older she called oldigers, and highlighted their strong work ethic.

Ages 40–53 she named holigers because they straddle the difference between the oldigers and the group she called the newigers (ages 28-40) who still have a good work ethic but want more in life than just work. She says that the newigers are the first generation whose clarity defined that work alone is not enough; they are looking for balance.

Those below age 28 she calls Synthesizers and declares them the Olympians of business; she believes our world is being led by them; she says they absorb information with lightening speed and that, even as children, they play with computers as though they were toys. Chandler says when she can get people ten to fifteen years old (who she still considers Synthesizers) on her team she relishes their feedback. "They have good perspective and insight for the future, and one can see the trends in thinking, products, and needs through them."

For all aspects of life, business, personal, and at all ages, it is important to set priorities, to have a plan for the way you approach each day. Go through the process of charting out your day in advance (include the various levels of importance in your life):

- work
- family
- relationships
- contribution

If you focus on one or two aspects and do not include all the things that are important, those things won't happen. If you wait to save your money until everything else has been paid, there may be none left. If you wait to spend time with your family or friends until after all the work is completed, you won't have much time with them.

You need free time to create, and you need to value that process enough to also set aside creative time regularly. It is just as important to reserve time to dream as it is to plan a specific event. Your planning will be more creative if you also have personal time scheduled, separately, when you can let creative ideas flow.

On the other hand, when you are working on a specific agenda, it is crucial that you do not lose sight of that as a primary priority; although creative dreaming is also a priority, getting sidetracked from the agenda is not. It is necessary to find that balance, to avoid the time robbers when you are in the midst of a project. The telephone is one of the offenders. People often allow the phone to interrupt current business for the hope of future business. My friend, Bob Proctor told me about a customer he observed at a hardware store. The customer was being waited on at the counter, but the phone rang, and the clerk stayed on the phone to answer questions for the potential customer while the actual customer waited patiently, but finally left without making his purchases. The storeowner called him later and asked why he left. The customer told him he couldn't understand why someone would ignore a purchase in front of you for the hope of a future one. (The old saying "a bird in the hand is worth two in the bush" applies here.)

Telephone tag is a common business occurrence, which has definitely contributed to much more busy-ness without outcome. With faxes, answering machines, voice mail, call waiting, teleconferencing, and email, we have more opportunities to contact people. However, we are likely wasting much more time waiting to actually make contact. With fax machines, there is an expectation by the sender that the recipient is miraculously at the other end, waiting in front of the machine to read and respond.

When I began to write this book and create the program, I incorporated it into the busiest quarter of my work schedule. The way you handle any big weight is with leverage—by adding big pulleys.

In allocating work, I ask myself the key questions:

- Who do I have to assist me?
- What am I doing?
- What am I doing that could be done by someone else?
- Why do I have to do that?

I should do nothing myself unless it is something my skill set must do. Otherwise, who do I have who could do this? It is all about priorities.

A change in momentum is based upon a shift in priorities. When you shift priorities, even for well-intentioned reasons, you will have a change in your habits. Most people who regularly fail to get things completed are guilty of redirecting their focus constantly; they don't stay focused to completion.

A shift in priorities is a change in habits due to a change in behavior. If you're working on a project, you go at it diligently for a month or so. While you're doing that, you gain momentum. The project takes on more life. When something else that seems more pressing takes your attention, you have to focus on that. If you don't recognize this shift in priorities, time will creep by—and your beloved project will dim. When you have stabilized your time and get back to that project, you are far more likely to use the time on something else. If you study people, that is why a lot of us don't get things done. People change their focus from one thing to another. Behavior is controlled by your subconscious mind. How many times have you decided to do something, set aside the time to do it, and didn't accomplish what you set aside the time to do? You function much more by habitual activity than you do by what you think in your conscious mind.

All things are possible, but it is a matter of thinking the way you have to think to do it. If I want to reduce the time in my medical practice in order to have more time to do other things, I have to look at my calendar in a three-year period and plan to reduce the office schedule by 12.5 percent for the first year, 12.5 percent the second year, and 12.5 percent the third year. At the same time, I have to plan another resource that will generate the money I will not be getting for that time.

The concept is **buying time**. It is setting up an incentive for the future. I must set up specific and generic breaks:

- Specific breaks are vacation,
- Generic breaks are certain other days that I may not work.

When you set generic breaks, if your subconscious mind is programmed for activity, you might find yourself doing lots of activities. They might not be your usual work activities, but your subconscious mind keeps on pushing you to use the time profitably.

Chapter 6

CURRENT TIME ISSUES

In our culture, everyone is pressed for time, concerned that we are poor time managers, and it is our fault. Surveys disclose that large percentages of people say they want more personal time, but most of them say it requires cutting back on sleep to make that time.

Why do we feel so time pressured? TV. We have an expanding volume of knowledge, mass media, and electronics addiction. TV is the biggest time waster, but it is being challenged by computers, online services, and social media. TV is the number one activity that steals your time—66 percent of Americans regularly watch TV while eating dinner, 49 percent say they watch TV too much, and 19 percent say they have no time to read and visit friends.

The average American watches more than four hours of TV each day, which equals two months of TV watching per year and more than twelve years in the life of a person who lives to age seventy-two.

TV is a drug. If you watch four hours of TV in two weekend nights, you have used eight hours of your life. The purpose of TV is not to entertain you; it is to sell you things. Ultimately, the quality of your life and your memories will depend upon on what you actively did—not what you passively ingested by seeing *Forrest Gump* for the third time. What will you do in the next month to enrich your life? Who will you meet? Where will you go? What will you risk? Who will you love? What will you learn?

Consider how much time and energy you are willing to spend with your favorite TV personality and contrast it with how much time you spend with any of your neighbors.

The number of minutes per week that parents spend in meaningful conversations with their children is 38.5. The number of minutes per week the average child spends watching TV is 1,680. Approximately 50 percent of children age 6–17 have a TV in their bedrooms, and 70 percent of day care centers use TV during a typical day. By age six, a child will have invested more hours watching TV than speaking with his or her father in an entire lifetime.

Knowledge is power, but how many people feel powerful in our country? Most Americans are under-informed, although the volume of new knowledge broadcast and published in every field is enormous. It exceeds anyone's ability to keep pace. All told, more words are published or broadcast in one day than you could comfortably ingest for the rest of your life. The impasse of this information overload era that confronts us is that the time necessary to learn all the rules for effective living now exceeds your life expectancy. This overload of what we can –or have to do—both in our personal and business lives -- often overwhelms people who already feel there is not enough time daily to do what has to be done. Some view it as impossible to address all of the new developments coming at us in a lifetime, feeling exhausted and frustrated with all of the new developments, rather than excited and interested. That is why it is important to sort out only what you feel is most important day to day, and only what you can accomplish in the time allotted that day. Most importantly, you must develop an attitude of sticking to that plan, not allowing yourself to be distracted by others, including those on TV, temptations of entertainment, or any of those who ask for "a minute of your time".

By far, the United States leads the world in the sheer volume of information generated and disseminated. That's why so many books **designed to help more readers be more effective in managing their time** fall so widely off the mark. They miss dozens, if not hundreds, of rules, and you already have so many rules for being effective in your career and in your life that you couldn't possibly keep track of them.

The key to winning back your time is to be more effective at "being", rather than "doing". In 1972, there were three major TV networks: ABC, NBC, and CBS. We now have channels specific to education, religion, entertainment, foreign language, weather, sports, arts, and lifestyle. Very shortly, there will be more than five hundred full-power independent TV stations, and many cable subscribers receive up to 140 channels that could offer 72,000 shows per month.

Americans today are consuming at least three times as much paper as they did ten years ago. The typical executive receives more than three hundred pieces of unsolicited mail each month and about twelve pieces daily. Annually, the average family receives more than two hundred catalogs they did not request—in addition to the ones they did request. We have an overabundance of choices. Unfortunately, having too many choices is like having too much of anything else. It leads to a feeling of being overwhelmed. Every choice demands time, and increased time expenditures result in mounting exhaustion.

Simply being born into this society at this time all but guarantees that you will increasingly feel more pressed for time. The more people there are, the more time-pressured you are. From the beginning of the creation of time to 1850, the world's population grew to one billion. It grew to two billion by 1930, three billion by 1960, four billion by 1979, and five billion by 1987. Currently it is around 7.5 billion. The United States population is 320 million, and there is a new birth in the United States every eight seconds. The more people, the more clog. It is as simple as that. There are more cars being built; they multiply twice as fast as people. So, there is bound to be gridlock. And now we are moving into cyberlock and airlock for sure; airline passenger traffic has more than tripled since 1980 and is growing by 7 percent annually, scheduled airlines carrying about 1 billion passengers last year. The United States is the largest market in the world in percentage of total scheduled passengers, domestic and international together.

When human beings are overexposed to stimuli, they feel a diminished sense of self-worth and self-esteem. Even people who set goals and do it well frequently feel overwhelmed. What hasn't been articulated in most books is the impact that so much information has on your sense of adequacy. More and more professionals feel inadequate. You don't necessarily need to slow down, but you do need to learn how to calm down. (Action Guide #21)

Nobody can keep on top of everything, but you can make choices about where you are going to direct your time and attention. The *New York Times* ran a major feature saying that people are experiencing stress and anxiety when shopping for leisure goods. There are so many choices; weighing such choices takes up your time, and the problem is even worse in the workplace. Every moment adds up. If you spend a lot of them contemplating which product or service to choose—from dozens or hundreds—you are consuming considerable amounts of time. Even when you choose wisely, it isn't once and for all. Next week, next month, or next year, a newer, better, faster, sleeker, less expensive, more powerful version of your product or service will be available.

Your unrelenting responsibility to keep choosing is a relatively unarticulated aspect of being born into this culture. Its cumulative effect is robbing you of your time. At first blush, it wouldn't seem that a plethora of choices is such a bad thing. After all, what can the harm be in having a wide variety of options? There is great harm in filling precious time with nagging, trivial decisions.

A wonderful technique for managing your time better is to become a consultant to yourself. Many people proceed through their days and their lives as if other people were in control of their time. When you are faced with too many choices, pretend you are a highly paid consultant to yourself. Proceed as if you are able to separate from your physical shell, move to the corner, and observe yourself from the vantage point of an objective third party. Refer to yourself in the third person. What does Joan/John need to do next? You derive different answers from those you get if you simply thought about what you should do next.

A semantic shift happens when you refer to yourself as if you were an observer. This practice opens a channel of discovery that is not readily available to you otherwise. Maybe it has to do with whether you are seeing the forest or the trees.

Chapter 7

LEVERAGING YOUR TIME

You can always make more money, but you can't make more time. I don't presume that you have loads of discretionary cash stashed away in a trunk. It's not likely that you have excess greenbacks lying around. This should go under leveraging your time with a time manager. Each time you avoid hiring a professional service or getting a helper, you are ensuring that you won't win back your time. A life manager or personal assistant equals time leveraging.

Reduce the info glut.

Do you lift your intellectual skirt willy-nilly and permit every newspaper, magazine, and newsletter publisher to sign you up? Take control of your money and your time. One equals the other.

You face so much that competes for your time and attention—your workaholic boss, an overfilled calendar, and future commitments. You'll need to think in terms of controlling the number of demands coming at you. Don't volunteer to have others hit you with even more requests that will compete for your attention. The effect of all of this is having too much to respond to, feeling overwhelmed, and having no sense of control over your time. The next time somebody calls to sell you on a highly worthwhile publication you can subscribe to, or needs a minute of your time, use what you have learned to politely decline.

Life Managers

People are trying to solve their time problems/challenges with various systems. Practical solutions are needed to handle these challenges. Leveraging time is a practical solution.

Don't do anything yourself that you can hire someone else to do. For every task in your life that someone else can do, you will save yourself for the tasks that only you can do and leverage your time. Why does it have to be done by me? I should never do something myself unless it is something my skill set must do. Who do I have who could do this?

- Make a list of some of the first things you would do if you had a life manager.
- Make a list of the things you would contract out.
- Nature abhors a vacuum. Create a space for the freedom you desire.
- Attract and secure a life manager.
    - Define what you are seeking in a helper (qualities, skill level, flexibility).
    - Create a job description to attract the kind of person you seek.
    - Check resources to identify your dream life manager.
    - Focus on what you want and what you're prepared to give. Identify the qualities and style you would need to become the sort of boss **you** would love to work for ---then sell the benefits of working for you.
    - Have the candidate fill out a personality profile.
    - Set up winning expectations of a one-minute manager, including an informative job description.
    - Set your life manager up to win right off the top.
- Develop a training schedule to avoid the shotgun approach.
- Create a detailed manual with your first life manager so that anyone else in the future can take over at warp speed.
- Be as clear as possible about goals and outcomes—and let them create the process.
- Create a structure for regular communication, especially if you will not be together frequently.
- Create a master workbook with categories for the diversity of things he/she will need to access: bank accounts, contact people, and routine appointments.
- Plan regular brief meetings in person and via phone to clarify targets and desired outcomes.
- Your big job in this is to let go of "how" it has to be done, and trust your life manager to get your defined outcomes. The clearer you are, the more easily they can please you.
- If you tell yourself you couldn't afford a personal assistant, you are fighting your old paradigm.
- You don't have to slow down, but you do have to calm down so that, in a confident manner, you can direct the traffic. (Action Guide 21)

Chapter 8

TURBO TIME

** Efficient Activity
** Chunking Projects
** Mind Mapping

COMPOUNDING YOUR OUTCOME

** Good Return on Your Time
Results Assessment

Busy people manage events—not time. As we have said, one doesn't really makes time because time just is. When you are multitasking, delegating, and doing things more effectively, you have the **perception** of having more time for yourself.

- Accomplish multiple goals within a unit of time.
- Don't multitask.
- Focus on doing more in a shorter time period with less effort.
- Set up multiple tasks simultaneously

Do all that can be done in an efficient manner. It is <u>not the number of things you do</u> but the efficiency of each action that counts. **Every efficient act is a success in itself**.

What do you get for the time you spend? With your time, you want a good return. If it is too big, hire someone to do the things that don't require your involvement—and focus on those that do.

What will your time buy?

What is your time is worth?

What is the price of your time? People will value your time only as much as the price you put on it.

Results are visible proof of the effectiveness of our thoughts and actions. They are feedback about our effectiveness. Constantly assess your results. Actions that lead to desired results should be reinforced through repetition. Unproductive actions should be discarded, and new plans should be constantly formed. Refine your actions to refine your results.

If I have to do something myself, when is the best time for me to do it? Can I piggyback the event onto something similar? Identify the six most important goal-achieving activities of each day, write them down, and vow to complete them before you go to bed. You, yourself, may not know the answers to these questions about yourself.

A truly evolved soul once suggested an exercise that was practiced thousands of years ago to determine what darkness was lurking in our deeper consciousness. The concept is based on **transferring thought and energy to an <u>inanimate</u> object**, giving the object life, and letting it tell you of itself, its views of the world and the energy around it. In modern terms, we would say that we are conveying our subconscious beliefs <u>about</u> that object <u>to</u> the object and letting it become conscious of itself **as part of our subconscious thinking**.

Using this ancient approach, then, this exploration of TIME may call for a "**conversation with your watch**". After all, as we have said, "watching that watch" is a major focus of our daily conscious existence. It's called Mind Mapping, and is directly attached to your consciousness of time. Since it is still within your consciousness, it should be able to tell you something about yourself.

For this exercise, please sit upright and get very relaxed. Close your eyes for a moment and release every pressing thought. Let go of all concerns and get yourself open and receptive to listen and understand what will evolve from your **subconcious**. Hold the watch and focus on it intently. Stare at that watch and tell it that you recognize that it represents spirit, substance, and form in your life. Tell it that it is alive and has a consciousness of itself, its importance in our world, and that it knows you best in your relationship to TIME.

Tell the watch that you are transferring your <u>subconscious</u> feelings and thoughts about time to it. In your mind's eye, feel or see a stream of energy flowing out of your solar plexus to the watch, totally saturating it with your feelings and beliefs about time.

To help you open the channels of communication, I am going to give you some questions to **ask** your watch. **Silently** ask the questions, listen to the responses that form in your mind, and write them down. Take a few seconds between questions to write down in your Action Guide section, **what you hear from your subconscious** so that, if you choose, you can go back over this exercise in greater depth, but let's practice now, listening to what the watch says to you.

Don't stop to analyze or evaluate what you hear—just write down your **immediate mental response:**

1. How would you describe my attitude toward you?
2. Do I fear you? And if so, why?
3. Have I ever abused you? And, if so, how?

For the next question, you will see a number flashing in your mind. Record the number on the paper.

4. On a scale of one to ten, one being the lowest and ten the highest, how would you measure my **integrity** as it specifically relates to **time**?
5. Do you feel that I am a **responsible** person regarding **time**?
6. What other information do you have for me regarding my **feelings** and **attitudes** toward **time**?

Take a good look at the responses, and you'll have an inside view of your hidden feelings. As we move on in the discussion of the principles of time abundance, any negative feelings will be transmuted through the positive energy of your new awareness, understanding, and knowledge of spiritual abundance.

The next chapter relates to **money and time** because the concepts are the same. I want to turn this exercise into a perception of time because we really view ourselves as not having enough time.

People think if they had enough money, they wouldn't be time scarce. Some people who have an awful lot of money actually have very little personal time to develop the things they want to do. Some people really have a good handle on it, but many don't. We tend to start with mechanisms and techniques instead of **consciousness about time**. We need to look at how we **think about time** before we start to manipulate the perimeters around it.

Chapter 9

TIME ABUNDANCE CONSCIOUSNESS

If you've experienced a source of time-lack in your life, it is because you have put the cart before the horse.

If you have a belief in lack and a belief in limitations, you have accepted the falsehood that lack is a normal part of your life. Isn't that ridiculous? But many of us run around trying to fill up that lack. We try to get money, wealth, abundance, and time. The consciousness of abundance must come before the physical manifestation of abundance.

Wealth is the result of consciousness—not the cause of it. Who or what we are speaks so loudly that sometimes we can't hear ourselves think. We are constantly picturing that which we believe we are and experiencing lack in our lives. We may say that we have faith in God, we may expect a miracle, or we may be almost able to convince ourselves that the all-good result is coming our way. However, an objective examination of the deep private side that we keep hidden from the world will bring to light old patterns of fear and doubt and our acceptance of lack as a natural state of being.

Time-Abundance Consciousness

- As Louise Hay tells us, "The work you are doing on yourself is not a goal. It is a process, a lifetime process. Enjoy the process." It is an important reminder when we are trying to revamp our approach to time.
- Awareness is the first step to change. Expansion is the goal. We sometimes have to change to expand, or intensify a current understanding to expand.
- The natural laws relate to time.
- Do all that can be done each day, and do each act in an efficient manner.
- Do not overwork or rush blindly in an effort to do the greatest possible number of things in the shortest amount time. You are not

to try to do tomorrow's work today or do a week's worth in a day. It is not the number of things you do but the efficiency of each separate action that counts. Every efficient act is a success in itself. Successful action is cumulative in its results.

- Every action is either strong or weak. Every act can be made strong and efficient by holding your vision while you are doing it and by putting the whole of your faith and purpose into it. Hold the vision of your outcome as you act.
- Success is achieved by doing enough things in an efficient manner and few things in an inefficient manner.
- When you begin to hurry, you cease being creative, and become competitive.
- Use positive time affirmations:
    - I work effectively at everything I do.
    - Time is my friend. I have all the time I need to accomplish my goals.
    - I have plenty of time today to handle all my important goals, personal relationships, and business.
    - The time I have is all the time I need to achieve outstanding results.
- People cheat themselves out of a lot because they don't take the time to see the value. **When you see the value, you'll have the time**.
- Change your concept of time to the truths known about time.
- Use your higher faculties, not your eyes. It is **perception** that counts. This is one of life's six intellectual factors.
- Align your time spent on any project with your values, basing it upon priorities you set.
- Dictate in which time frames you will accomplish things.
- **You have all the time you need**.
- **The time frame is here and now—everywhere and anywhere you are (no matter what time zone you are in)**
- **Expect to have a life filled with times orchestrated through goals and values** and a delegated support system so your life is the way you want it to be. You can insist on it by going toward your vision and seeing it consciously.
- Provide more service (produce something of value that people want) in less time through effective action principles.

- We need more money all the time. The core of your being is always for expansion and forward expression toward spirit. Spirit cannot express itself as fully through you if you don't expand your resources.
- You have to create financial resources to have more available time to direct the experiences you are looking for.
- We leverage our time and effort by thinking
- **It is what you do—not what you know—that counts**. In fact, it is what you do with what you know that's important.
- Conscious, competent people add joy to their productivity (the result of producing more in less time)
- Have an attitude of gratitude. Appreciate and focus on the moments when you do activities you love with people you love. **We attract more of what we focus on most.** By orchestrating your time through effective management of activities and events, you create more powerful outcomes in less time. This leaves you more time to enrich other people's lives. ****The platinum rule is to treat others as they want to be treated, not as you think they should be treated. (see *The Platinum Rule* by Dr. Tony Alessandra and Dr. Michael O'Connor.

Chapter 10

MANIFESTATION

To manifest is to materialize. The process of manifestation is to concentrate thought energy on the no-thing (universal mind, the unified field, spirit). And through our actions—while concentrating on whatever we are focused on—it will ultimately become manifested in the material realm. There are levels of energy from the invisible, which vibrate so quickly we cannot see them in our three-dimensional world, continuing down to things that vibrate more slowly so we can see them. **Thought is a higher order of vibration** than something concrete. Our goal as humans, with choice, is to find ways to manifest from invisible thoughts to the material realm in more effective ways.

Wallace Wattles says, "There is a thinking stuff from which all things are made, and which, in its original state, permeates, penetrates, and fills the interspaces of the universe." A thought in this substance produces the thing that is imaged by the thought. A person can form things in thoughts, and impressing the thoughts upon formless substance, can cause the thing to be created. In order to do this, people must pass from the competitive to the creative mind. They must form a clear picture of the thing they envisioned mentally and hold this picture in their thoughts with a fixed purpose to get what they want, with an unwavering faith that they will get it. Closing the mind to any possibilities of it may shake their purpose, dim their vision, or quench their faith.

We can blend science with spiritual explanations. All material creation has the same origin. Nature goes to the same place to create a cluster of nebulas, a galaxy of stars, an ocean, a human body, or a thought. All material creation, anything that has been manifested, comes from the same source. **Our goal is to create material reality out of a nonmaterial essence**.

According to quantum theorists, all material things are made up of atoms, which are comprised of subatomic particles, which are fluctuations of energy and information in a huge void of energy and information. **The basic conclusion of quantum field theorists is that the raw material of the world**

is non-material. The essential stuff of the universe is non-stuff. All of our technology is based upon this fact.

Computers, fax machines, televisions, and other tangible things we see and use in our three-dimensional world have been manifested because scientists no longer believe that the atom is a solid entity. An atom is a hierarchy of states of information and energy in a void of all possible states of information and energy.

The difference between one material thing and another is not on a material level. Subatomic particles comprise the atoms. The protons, electrons, quarks, and bosons that make up an atom of gold or an atom of wood, are the same. Although we call them particles, they are not material things. They are impulses of energy and information. What makes gold different from wood is the arrangement and quantity of these impulses of energy and information. In fact, all quantum events are basically fluctuations of energy and information. This essential stuff of the **universe is non-stuff**, and it is **thinking non-stuff**.

What else are thoughts but impulses of energy and information occurring in our heads? We experience them as linguistically structured, but those impulses of energy and information are the raw material of the universe. At a preverbal level (prior to speech/language), all of nature speaks the same language. **We are all thinking bodies in a thinking universe**.

Physicists tell us that we go beyond the realm of subatomic particles and into the cloud of subatomic particles that make up the atom. As we try to examine and understand these quarks, bosons and leptons, the particles are too small to measure. In fact, they are so small that we can only think about them. They have never been seen. How do we know they exist? They leave evidence in particle accelerators. **These subatomic particles come into existence only when we observe them**. **In other words, every time we look at these particles, they blink into existence**. **When we turn our attention away, they disappear into a void**. They blink on and off like lights in a dark room. If you imagine the dark room as infinite, the particles that blink into existence do so by the mere act of our putting our attention of thought into the field.

Each particle is only a wave until the moment it is observed. A wave is not restricted to any one location in space or time. It is a diffuse thing; and because of this it is termed a probability amplitude in the field of all possibilities. Wikipedia defines a probability amplitude as a complex number used in describing the behavior of systems. **It merely defines statistically the likelihood of finding a particle at a specific place at just the time**

your attention was placed on the no-thing. A particle is literally created by you through the act of observation. All material creation is nothing but the self, experiencing itself, through different qualities of its own attention to itself. **Attention** is the very mechanics of turning a space-time event into the no-thing; it brings it into our awareness and into our lives in its material expression.

Scientists have shown that mental events transform themselves into molecules that permeate every cell of the body. Thinking a thought is brain chemistry and body chemistry. Every thought you entertain sends chemical messages to the core of cellular awareness. Putting attention on a word, which is the symbolic expression of an idea, is a miracle. It transforms the invisible into the visible. **You get what you think about most. By directing your thoughts, you manage your outcomes.**

There are natural laws that govern the universe. The philosophical conception of natural law first appeared among ancient Greek thinkers, such as Plato and Aristotle, ultimately moving (as presented in Wikipedia) from divine rights to certain rights and values that are inherent by virtue of human nature and are universally cognizable through human reason. **They further state that natural law is the uniform and orderly method of the omnipotent God or the omnipotent energy (if it is viewed scientifically).**

English philosopher John Locke focused on three natural rights that he related to governing and government as rights innate to all human beings: life, liberty, and estate. Wallace Wattles addresses these natural laws in *The Science of Getting Rich*, and Napoleon Hill does it in *Think and Grow Rich*. From the many observations of the universal laws discussed in Wikipedia, **it appears that one great law emerged: energy.** All physical and mental science is based on this one great law and its seven subsidiary laws, which I have listed below. The seven subsidiary laws exist to support the one great law. They have no particular hierarchical order. They exist and operate simultaneously all the time.

The Law of Perpetual Transmutation

- Energy moves into physical form.
- The images you hold in your mind most often materialize as results in your life.

The Law of Relativity

- Nothing is good or bad or big or small until you relate it to something.
- Practice relating your situation to something much worse, and yours will look good.

The Law of Vibration

- Everything vibrates, and nothing rests.
- Conscious awareness of vibration is called feeling. Your thoughts control your paradigms and your vibration.
- When you are not feeling well, become aware of what you are thinking—and then think of something pleasant.

The Law of Polarity

- Everything has an opposite: hot/cold, up/down, good/bad.
- Constantly look for the good in people and situations. When you find it, tell them. People love compliments, and the positive idea in your mind makes you feel good. Remember, good thoughts bring good vibrations.

The Law of Rhythm

- The tide comes in, and the tide goes out. Night follows day. Good times follow bad times.
- When you are on a downswing, do not feel bad. The swing will change. Think of the good times ahead.

The Law of Cause and Effect

- Whatever you send into the universe comes back. Say good things to everyone. Action and reaction are equal and opposite.
- Treat everyone with total respect, and it will come back. Never worry about what you will get. Concentrate on what you can give.

The Law of Gender

- Every seed has a gestation or incubation period. Ideas are spiritual seeds and will move into form or physical results.
- Your goals will manifest when the time is right. Know they will.

It is not the intention of this program to delve more deeply into these phenomena, but if they are of interest to you, I encourage you to study them. Bob Proctor deals with them in many of his programs, particularly in *The Science of Getting Rich.* Deepak Chopra has a book and a video called *The Seven Spiritual Laws.* Many other learned people have expounded upon these principles.

Manifestation as a process, and understanding the rules, varies greatly in our experience. Since we have a finite amount of time on the planet in one incarnation, we want to become experts at manifestation. **In a spiritual context, time is timeless and infinite. There is no time or space.**

We belong to a multidimensional universe, but so much of our consciousness is focused on the three-dimensional world in which we live. But what does that really mean? A dimension is a mode of existence; the number of dimensions denotes the directional potentialities inherent in the mode of existence. The first dimension is the element of length. The second dimension comprises the elements of length and width. The third dimension, the earthy realm, comprises the elements of length, width, and depth, and its inhabitants are physical beings. The fourth dimension comprises the elements of length, width, depth, and time. The fifth dimension has the elements of length, width, depth, time, and spirituality. **There are at least twenty dimensions, but the elements beyond the third dimension are not physical, concrete entities. They are states of consciousness. We can each live on any number of different planes, depending on the plane our spiritual experiences have reached.**

Since this program is about time, let us talk about the fourth dimension for a moment. **For two objects to come into contact with each other in the <u>third dimension</u>, they both have to exist simultaneously at the same time of the same day of the same week of the same year, but this is not true in the <u>fourth dimension</u>**. Two people shaking hands might not belong to the same era at all. In the fourth dimension, it would be perfectly possible for a person of the present day to shake hands with someone from the tenth century. Sound a little like *Star Trek*? No wonder we have so much difficulty managing time. How can we hope to manage an entity that does not really exist on the three-dimensional plane in which our physical bodies live? Time cannot be managed. Nobody manages time. Effective people manage events—not time.

It is only in this very moment that we experience anything. In the next moment, the moment we just experienced is in the past. The moment just ahead is in the future. It is in the delicate balance of focus on future moments that dreams and plans occur, but we can only execute events in this moment, The Here and Now. In our consciousness, we skip backward, forward, and to the now in an instant. Plans are developed by projecting our thoughts to a future thinking or creating something from the no-thing and bringing it forward to the now to actually create something from nothing. This whole process of manifestation or creation can take us as little as a few moments up to hundreds of years.

Any thought that you intend to transmute to the physical equivalent must be planted in the subconscious mind, come through your creative imagination, and be mixed with the emotion of faith. Your subconscious mind is most receptive to reprogramming the first thing in the morning upon arising or just before sleep.

There are four basic steps in manifesting anything:

- **Build the image through the sixth sense, creative imagination.**
- **Get emotionally involved by using the other five senses to emotionally experience the event now.**
- **Have faith that spirit will lead. Some people say, "Let go and let God."**
- **Expect abundance and walk with an attitude of gratitude as though you have already received what you seek. It will only be a matter of time before your thought is manifested on the three-dimensional plane.**

Manifestation means to materialize. All material creation has the same origin. It is called by many names, depending upon your cultural, philosophical, religious, or spiritual background. Some call it the no-thing, Universal Intelligence, or Spirit.

There is this thinking stuff from which all things are made and which, in its original state permeates, penetrates, and fills the interspaces of the universe.

The process of thinking about something is the necessary path to its manifestation, the beginning for creating the thing we thought about.

By putting our attention through a thought, we materialize the thing we thought about.

It may take moments or centuries to bring an idea from the immaterial to the three-dimensional material world, but the process of manifestation is the same.

Any thought you intend to transmute to the physical equivalent must be planted in the subconscious mind, come through your imagination, and be mixed with faith.

The Process of Manifestation/Creation

- Go into a relaxed, meditative state.
- Build the image through the sixth sense, creative imagination, to access spirit/universal energy.
- Get emotionally involved with the image. (Create a high vibration.)
- Have faith that spirit will lead. (Let go and let God.)
- Expect abundance. (Attitude of gratitude.)

Creative energy will attract ideas, people, and circumstances toward you, which will coalesce into the combinations necessary to create the outcome about which you have been dreaming.

What we see is clearly a function of our point of observation.
—Albert Einstein

TIME-LIBERATION ACTION GUIDE

EXERCISES

Take charge of the time in your life. This is your life. Time is the most valuable expenditure you will ever make in your life. Time is precious. Make your time count.

The concepts and laws incorporated into this program are universal. They will work for every person. *On Time* is designed to transform your thoughts and behaviors about time pressure and time scarcity to time-abundance consciousness.

Being born into this society at this time all but guarantees that you will feel pressed for time. We live in the **age of time famine**.

Schools focus on imparting information. Business courses focus on efficiency. *On Time* focuses on effectiveness.

Most people try to solve their time problems with time-management systems. They work at trying to be more efficient, but time cannot be managed.

Our goal is to help you to see the way to solution through effective thoughts and actions about time. It begins with your consciousness, developing a time-abundance consciousness.

Prepare yourself for the time <u>of</u> your life. This is the most effective program on time in the world today. It is a paradigm-shifting program that gives you the critical tools necessary to

---

TAKE CHARGE OF THE TIME <u>IN</u> YOUR LIFE

Action Guide 1

Rate yourself from 1 to 10 on the way you presently feel about time.
Time
Scarcity 0——————————5—————————————10 abundance

List at least five words to describe how you feel about time.

____

____

____

Describe what your life would be like if you were a 10 on the time-consciousness continuum.

____

____

____

List at least five words to describe how you would feel if you had TIME ABUNDANCE CONSCIOUSNESS____________________

As a result of rating your attitudes and the words you use to describe how you feel about time, what have you learned about yourself?

____

Is there anything about your time attitude you would like to modify? What and how?______________________________

____

____

____

"The work you are doing on yourself is not a goal. It is a process—a lifetime process. Enjoy the process." Louise Hay

---

Action Guide #2

Only One Source of Supply

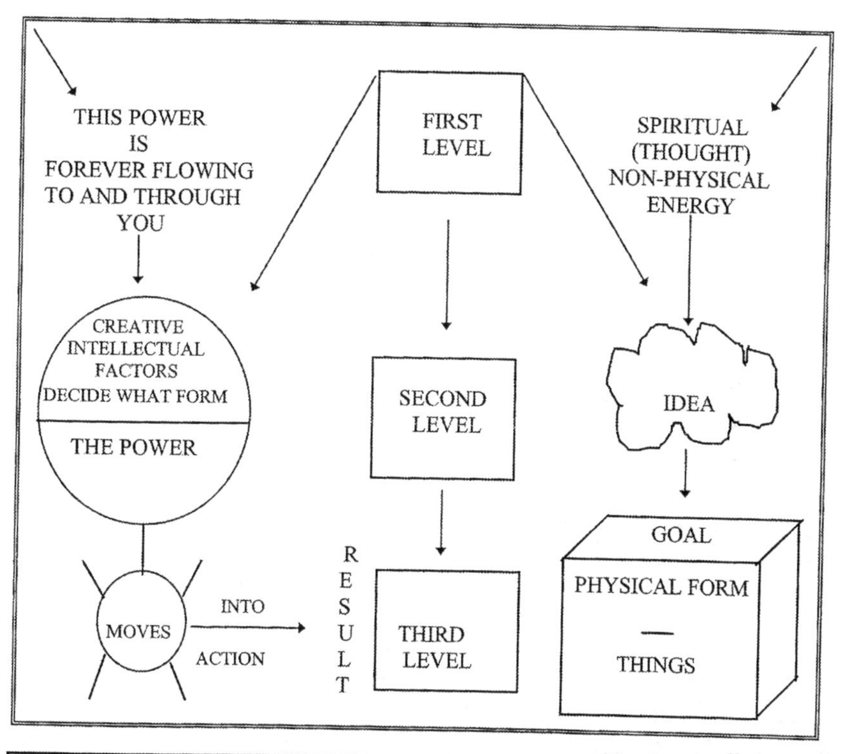

> "What we see is clearly a function of our point of observation."
> Albert Einstein

<u>Mental faculties</u>

<u>Concrete Faculties</u>
<u>The Five Sensory Factors</u>

Use these to stay in touch with the Physical World

1. Sight
2. Sound
3. Smell
4. Taste
5. Touch

<u>Creative Faculties</u>
<u>The Six Intellectual Factors</u>

Use these to Build goals

1. Reason
2. Will
3. Perception
4. Memory
5. Intuition
6. Imagination

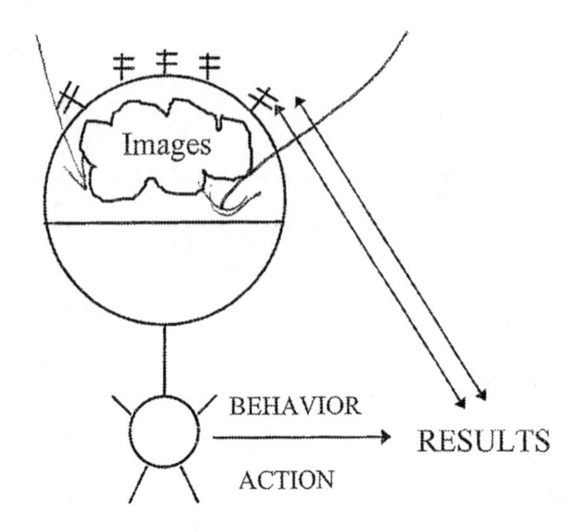

Although the five senses are beneficial because they are the faculties through which we communicate with the outside world, they are also limited because they keep us focused on our current results rather than on using our creative imaginations to build images of our dreams.

The Sixth Sense: Creative Imagination

The faculty of creative imagination is an intellectual factor used regularly by children, but a relatively small number of adults use it deliberately and with purpose. We call these people GENIUSES . All so-called revelations referred to in religion—and all new discoveries and inventions—take place through creative imagination. CREATIVE IMAGINATION IS THE DIRECT LINK BETWEEN THE FINITE MIND OF MAN AND SPIRIT.

The Logical Mind

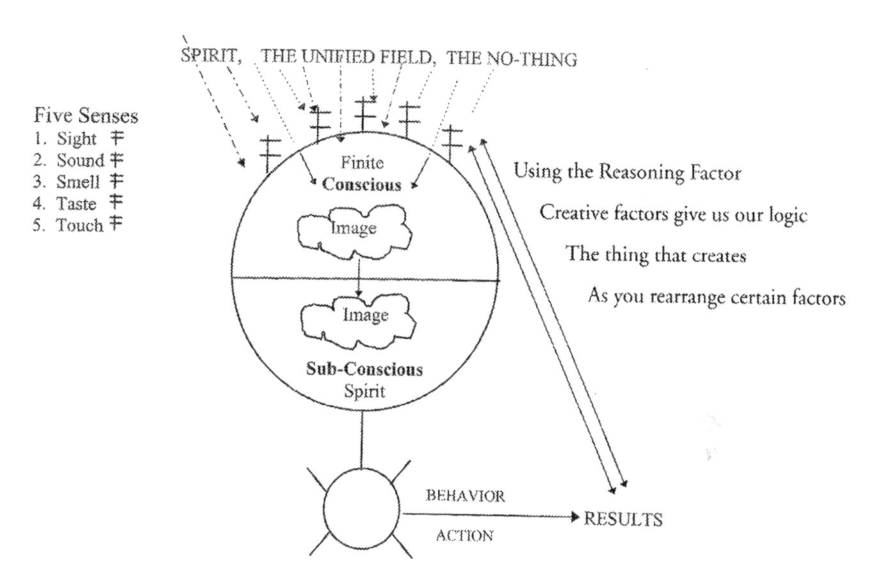

We have glorified the logical, scientific approach, particularly in Western culture. We have adopted phrases like "seeing is believing." The typical paradigm on this planet is that we react to what we see, hear, smell, taste, and touch by interpreting and judging our results and getting emotionally involved with our judgments. We then try to change things as a reaction to our current results by changing the images inside our heads. This process is a **deductive-reasoning process**.

We also use our six intellectual factors to pull in a new image that is not based upon current results. We wish for something more or better from the unified field (the no-thing or spirit consciousness). Unfortunately, we rarely sustain the new image because we are habituated to looking at our current results and our judgments of them to create our next thoughts. Thus, the logical mind is a judgment loop. While this deductive reasoning process can be helpful in a problem-solving capacity, it is an ineffective process for manifestation.

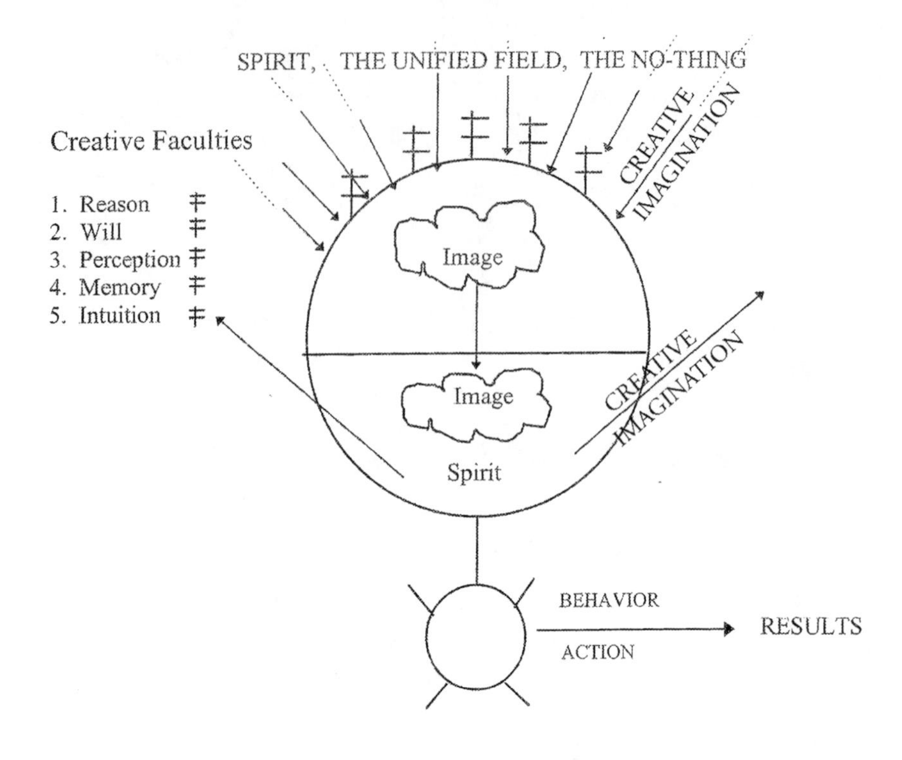

The Creative Mind

There are six intellectual factors, and these are the characteristics that separate us as human beings from the rest of the animal kingdom. The six creative faculties give us a direct link between our own finite minds and spirit (the unified field, the no-thing). Through the process of mediation, we have a precise mechanism through which all desires can be manifested. We begin by relaxing and paying no attention to our current results. Rather, in a meditative state, we use creative imagination to build the images of what we want. We then detach emotionally from the need to have it, trusting that the way will be shown to lead to action, which will cause us to manifest our desired result. In the gap between what we want and our trust of detachment from the "how", the answer will come.

Action Guide 3

Time Freedom

The past does not equal the future unless you say so. If **time scarcity** has been a challenge for you in the past, it does not have to be in your future.

Time freedom can be your future.

You need to make distinctions about where you have been up until now. Are you are satisfied with that perspective? Do you believe a shift or change in your time consciousness is in your best interests?

A lot of your willingness to work on changing your perspective and behaviors about time—even when you see the benefits of doing so—depends upon **your emotional flexibility about change** in general.

CHANGE CAN BE:

- a joyous journey
* a laborious effort
* an impossible obstacle

Which one will you choose, CONSIDERING YOUR RELATIONSHIP TO TIME?

____

____

____

When we are ready to make positive changes in our lives, we attract whatever we need to help us.

—Louise Hay

Action Guide 4

Soon the life expectancy for women is expected to be eighty-five, and the life expectancy for men is expected to be seventy-nine. In 1900, women generally lived to be forty-eight, and men lived to be forty-six.

Based on your family history, the way you take care of yourself, your energy and desire for life, and your beliefs about your own life force, how old do expect to live? _____Years

With decades to go, it is easy to get caught in the trap of delaying the activities and events you promised yourself you would undertake.

In what percent of your time are you fully engaged with vitality? _____%
In what percent of your time would you **like** to be fully engaged? _____%

There are 168 hours (10,080 minutes) available for your expenditure each week.
Record the number of hours and minutes you spend in a typical week on the following activities:

Hrs / Minutes
family ________________________________
spouse _____ __________________________
children ______________________________
community/friends ____________________
contribution to society__________________(Volunteering/Helping others)
spiritual_______________________________
personal growth________________________
work__________________________________
work catch up__________________________
TV/passive_____________________________
sports/active___________________________
entertainment__________________________
home/personal__________________________
maintenance____________________________
projects_______________________________

Action Guide 4 Cont'd

What do you notice about how you spend your time?

____

____

____

____

____

What would you like to do more of/less of and how much?

____

____

____

____

Are there any activities you would like to delegate to someone else? If so, which ones?

____

____

____

____

> Doest thou love life? Then do not squander time,
> for that's the stuff life is made of.
> —Benjamin Franklin

Action Guide 5

People often say, "If I just had more time." Everybody gets the same amount of time in one_day—24 hours. Some people use their time more effectively, some people experience more fun and joy, and some people get a greater return on their time or make more money. **But make no** mistake: **Everybody gets the same amount of time to create an outcome**.

PEOPLE USE, LOSE, AND ABUSE TIME ALL THE TIME.

Historically, Schools focus on imparting information, business courses focus on efficiency.

***On Time* focuses on time effectiveness**.

Effective people successfully manage the events in their lives. They do not create effective outcomes by accident.

EFFECTIVE PEOPLE ARE RESULTS ORIENTED AND FOCUS ON GOALS.

Name your most important goals.--
Name the ones you have already reached.-----------------------------------

> Successful people are not any smarter than anyone else. They have simply learned to use what they have effectively.
> —Bob Proctor

Action Guide #6
Time Cannot Be Managed

Nobody manages time. People can manage events or at least their reactions to events, but nobody manages time. There are hundreds of "time-management" programs that seek to make you more efficient—as though that is the solution. Time-efficiency activities can be helpful, but these programs are dealing with the **symptoms** of time pressure rather than the **root cause** (the way you think and behave about time).

We all know the world is changing, and people are beginning to be paid for what they do—rather than what they know. This is heartwarming for effective people. Make your goal the development of time-abundance consciousness and the study and modeling of effective behavior.

Effective behavior is the key. It is based upon the way you think and behave about time.

In times of change, the learners will inherit the earth,
while the learned will find themselves beautifully equipped
to deal with the world that no longer exists.
—Eric Hoffer

Action Guide 7

Ineffective behaviors/activities in which I routinely engage:

____
____
____
____
____
____
____
____

Effective behaviors/activities in which I routinely engage:

____
____
____
____
____
____
____
____

Action Guide #8

Describe how you feel about your repetitive ineffective behaviors?

____
____
____
____

Describe how you feel about your repetitive effective behaviors?

Will you choose to add to or subtract from any of your lists? If so, which ones?

Is there one effective behavior not on your list that you know will increase your success dramatically if you set a goal to add it to your repertoire of behaviors? What is it? Will you do it? If yes, when and how?

Action Guide #9

In one sentence, summarize the essence of what you learned about yourself regarding taking responsibility for time in your life.

Record the effective behavior you will concentrate on for the next forty days. Record how this affects your day. Decide now on the reward you will give yourself at the end of the forty days for successfully completing this commitment.

Action Guide #10

Rate yourself from 1 to 10 on the way you presently feel about change.

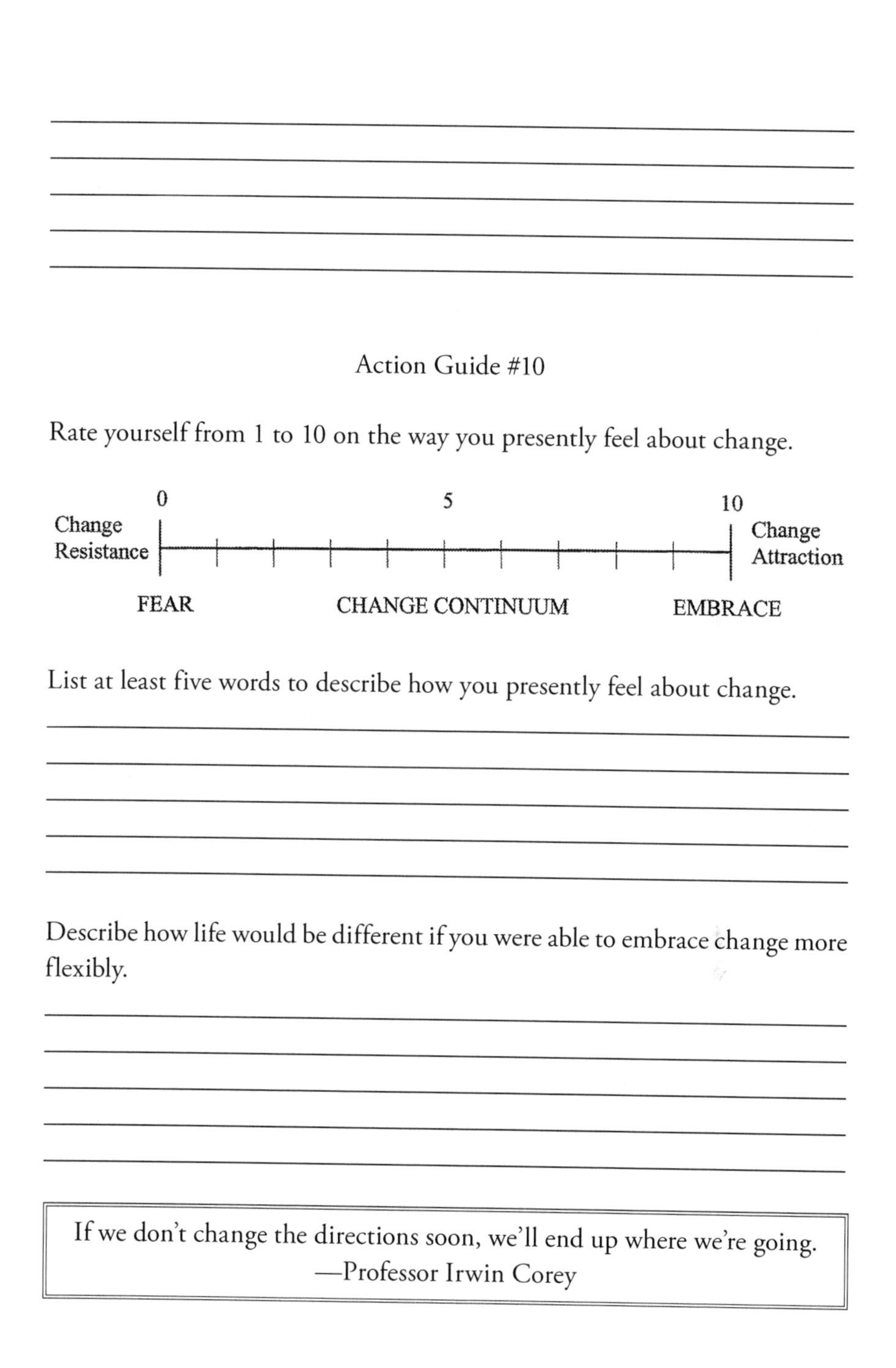

List at least five words to describe how you presently feel about change.

Describe how life would be different if you were able to embrace change more flexibly.

> If we don't change the directions soon, we'll end up where we're going.
> —Professor Irwin Corey

Action Guide #11

VISUALIZING THE MIND (The Stick Person Concept)

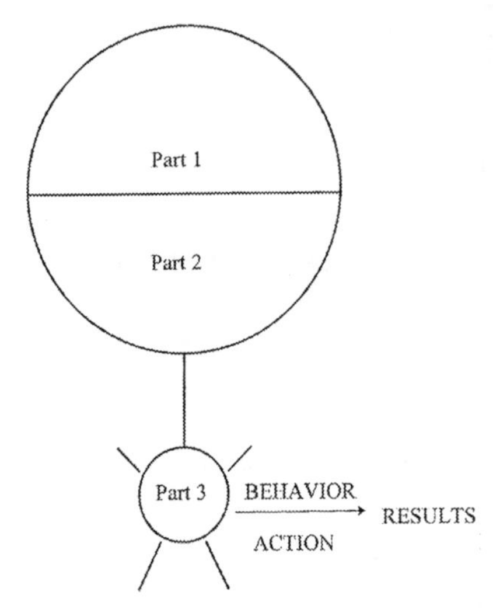

In the conscious mind (part 1), thoughts come in actively or passively. The conscious mind accepts or rejects the ideas.

- You generate **active thoughts consciously**.
- **Passive thoughts are generated outside you** and are taken in unconsciously or uncritically from stimuli such as other people, TV, radio, or newspapers.

When the **conscious mind** (part 1 in the drawing) **accepts** any thought, either actively or passively, **it is automatically impressed on the subconscious mind**, as part of your personality. (Part 2 in the drawing)

The subconscious mind accepts all information that was not rejected by the conscious mind and creates vibrations/feelings that move through the Body (Part 3), as actions or behaviors.

The body is an instrument of the mind, the house in which you live. It creates the physical actions/behaviors that lead to results.

"Mind" is in every cell of your body

Action Guide #12

The Conscious Mind

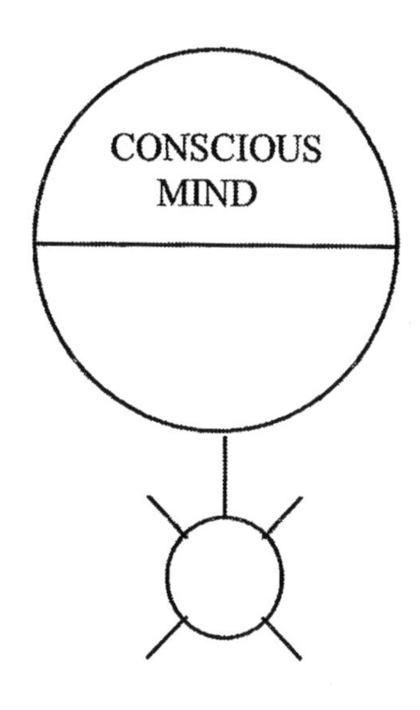

This is the part of you that thinks and reasons; your free will lies here. The conscious mind can accept or reject any idea. No person or circumstance can cause you to think about thoughts or ideas you do not choose. The challenge is to stay alert at the door of your mind. When you do not actively choose your focus, the conscious mind can receive data not generated by you and passively take it in. THE THOUGHT YOU CHOOSE WILL EVENTUALLY DETERMINE THE RESULTS OF YOUR LIFE. All pain, pleasure, and limitations originate in the conscious mind or are accepted uncritically from an outside source.

Action Guide 13

The Subconscious Mind

This is the power center, the most magnificent part of who you are. It is your SPIRIT, the godlike part of you. It knows no limits. Since it only accepts ideas and has no ability to reject, every thought your conscious mind has accepted actively or passively will be seen as its truth in that moment.

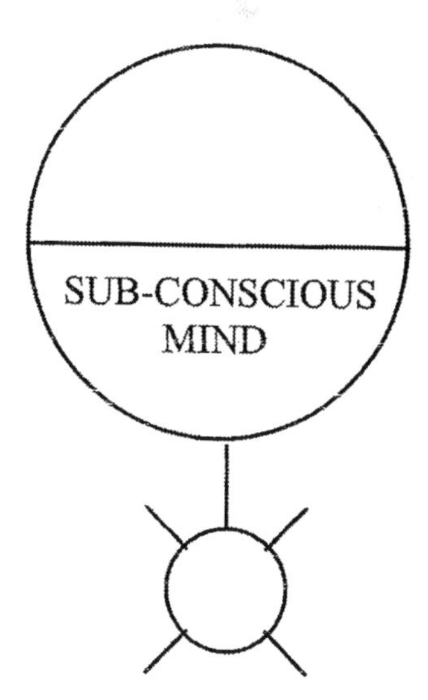

The subconscious mind works in an orderly manner. By "law", it expresses itself through your feelings and actions. Any thought you consciously or unconsciously impress through repetition on the subconscious mind becomes fixed inside this part of your personality. Once ideas are fixed, they continue to express themselves automatically as habits, and**, they require no conscious thoughts to initiate and/or sustain them.**

Once information is programmed into your subconscious, whether it is resourceful or non-resourceful, **even when you consciously want to change it**, you can only do so through repetition of the new idea until the old habit is reprogrammed.

Choose your thoughts carefully. You become what you think about.

Action Guide 14

The BODY

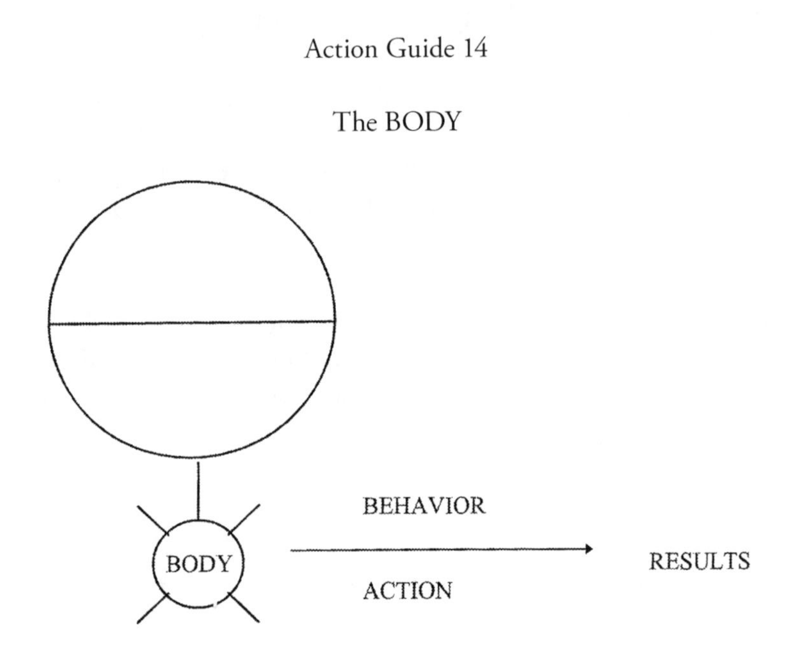

Although this is the most obvious part of you, it is the smallest part. The body is the physical presentation of you, the material medium. It is an instrument of the mind. The thoughts or images you consciously and unconsciously choose are impressed upon the subconscious mind. Once in the subconscious mind, this image moves through your body as behavior or action. Action leads to results.

Get all three parts of your personality working in harmony to win. To improve your circumstances, you must improve yourself.

Action Guide #15

REPROGRAMMING
(The Process of Change)

Let go of the past. Once habits are formed, whether resourceful or non-resourceful, they are your paradigm, the mirror through which you see everything. The pull to sustain habits is strong, even when your conscious mind wants to create a change. The doubts, fears, and anxieties you experience are not the result of a lack of potential. They are the result of inferior conditioning in your subconscious mind. You must cross a **terror barrier** to change.

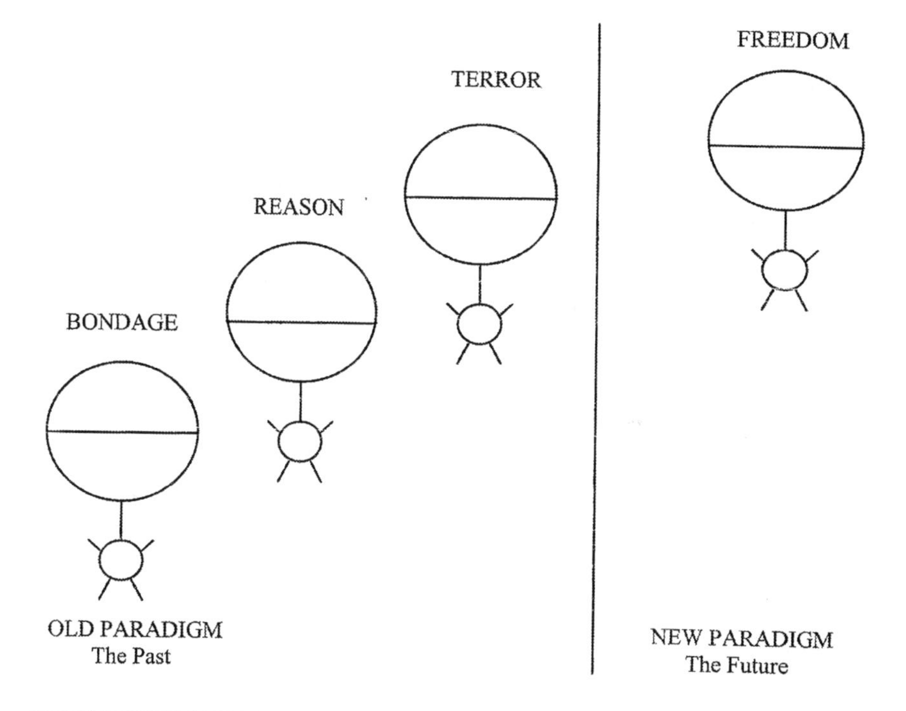

> You will either step forward into growth, or you will step back into safety.
> —Abraham Maslow

Action Guide 16

Do you think you have to have money to have TIME FREEDOM? Money gives you easier access to freedom, including time freedom, but it does not guarantee it. In fact, there are plenty of people with a lot of money who do not experience time freedom because they still have a time-slavery consciousness. **They trade time for money**. They make a lot of money, but it takes a lot of time to do it––and they work all the time.

Circle one of the three choices about time freedom that most accurately reflects your attitude about it:

- Desirable
- Important
- Essential

Use your consciousness in a positive way. **Elevate your wants to musts**!

If you chose desirable or important rather than essential, what will stop you from elevating it to essential?

____
____
____
____
____
____

Action Guide 17

Check the answers that most accurately apply to your feelings.

I feel rushed:

Never	Infrequently	Rarely	Regularly	Frequently	Usually	Always
❑	❑	❑	❑	❑	❑	❑

I feel controlled by events outside myself:

Never	Infrequently	Rarely	Regularly	Frequently	Usually	Always
❑	❑	❑	❑	❑	❑	❑

I choose an attitude of time freedom:

Never	Infrequently	Rarely	Regularly	Frequently	Usually	Always
❑	❑	❑	❑	❑	❑	❑

I am responsible for my attitude about time:

Never	Infrequently	Rarely	Regularly	Frequently	Usually	Always
❑	❑	❑	❑	❑	❑	❑

Are you working every day on the effective behavior you want to add? (Refer back to Guides 9 and 10 to review your answers regarding your commitment to taking responsibility to Time

Action Guide 18

A Sense of Urgency

A sense of urgency is being able to automatically detect goal-achieving projects that call for immediate attention and acting on them until they are successfully completed.

Nothing makes a person more productive than the last minute.

There are so many events and distractions that one could constantly be in motion and yet accomplish very little. A Sense Of Urgency **used in a resourceful way** can help you focus your energy and cut through a lot of extraneous information to direct you toward resolution and a solution.

DEVELOPING A SENSE OF URGENCY INTO A HABIT IS A PROJECT IN ITSELF AND A WORTHWHILE INVESTMENT OF YOUR TIME.

Individuals with a sense of urgency always have a lot to do; they know they will get it done, and they complete their projects in a calm, confident manner.
They are professionals.
—Bob Proctor

Action Guide 19

GETTING THINGS DONE

The world has always cried out for men and women who can get things done, people who are self-starters, and those who see a task through to its completion. These are the **producers of the world**. THEY CHANGE THE WORLD'S STANDARD OF LIVING, and THEY WIN THE BIG SHARE WORLD'S REWARDS.

People who fail to make their lives great know what to do, and they **almost** do it on time. The "almosts" are not lazy. Often they are busier than the effective few. They often putter around all day long and half the night, but they fail to accomplish important tasks. The "almosts" are frequently held back by indecision, lack of organization, and too much attention to minor details

PRODUCERS, on the other hand, **have a fine-tuned sense of urgency**.

"Seest thou a person diligent in their business?
They shall stand before kings."
—Proverbs 22:29

Action Guide 20

THE LAW OF CAUSE AND EFFECT

Producers understand the law of cause and effect. There is no such thing as service without reward, and producers understand how this applies to everything in life.

This law applied to money is known as the law of compensation, and the amount of money you earn will always be in direct ratio to:

- the need for what you do
- your ability to do it
- the difficulty there will be in replacing you

Focus all your attention on **your ability to do it**. Become more effective and professional, and you will find that the other two requirements are taken care of automatically.

Rate yourself from 0 to 10 about how you see yourself in this category.

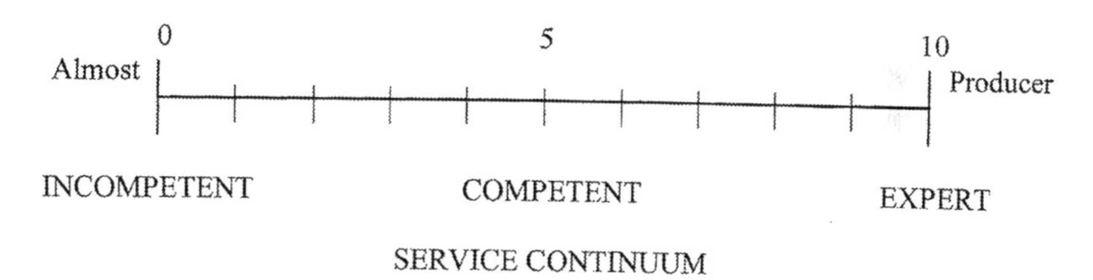

Describe how you feel about your compensation, based upon how you rated yourself.

____

____

____

____

____

Action Guide 21

You do not have to learn how to slow down, but you have to learn how to calm down.

Formula for Success: Take Action, holding the vision with will power, that your desired outcome will be strong, efficient, and effective, putting your whole faith and expectancy and purpose into it.

When you have a big project to complete with no established due date, do you have a typical way to pace yourself? Describe it below.

____
____
____
____
____
____
____

If you have several projects facing you simultaneously, how do you pace the work? Describe it below:

____
____
____
____
____
____
____

> Works expands so as to fill the time available for its completion.
> —Cyril Northcote Parkinson

Action Guide 22

Describe how you feel about your work habits and style of approaching projects.

____
____
____
____
____

Is there someone with whom you are associated or whose work with which you are acquainted who is a master of project management? Name that person.

What have you noticed about how he or she approaches work? What behaviors could you mimic to be more effective?

____

____

____

____

____

____

____

What single behavior exhibited by your chosen Master of Project Management do you feel would benefit you most if you adopted it or enhanced it?

____

____

____

____

____

____

> Experience is not what happens to a man; it is what
> a man does with what happens to him.
> —Aldous Huxley

Action Guide 23

When someone asks, "Do you have a minute?" it is a request for your time that usually is not tailored to <u>your</u> needs, nor probably even to help solve the other person's problem. It is more likely an open-ended invitation to **voice a complaint**.

Five minutes wasted here and there all day long adds up to an hour. One hour per day for one year equals nine forty-hour weeks. That is a lot of time, which—if used resourcefully—could change the quality of your future.

Your life is a series of connected events, about many of which you can exercise responsible, directed choices. Remain conscious of how you invest your moments.

People usually **overestimate what they can accomplish in one year** and **underestimate what they can accomplish in five years**. Make big plans and take action on them regularly. Commit yourself to constant and never-ending improvement.

COMPOUND YOUR TIME EFFECTIVELY

> When I look back on all these worries, I remember the story of the old man who said on his deathbed that he had a lot of trouble in his life—most of which never happened.
> —Sir Winston Churchill

Action Guide 24

Check the answers that most accurately reflect your feelings.

I criticize/complain:

Never	Infrequently	Rarely	Regularly	Frequently	Usually	Always
❑	❑	❑	❑	❑	❑	❑

I listen to other people criticize/complain:

Never	Infrequently	Rarely	Regularly	Frequently	Usually	Always
❑	❑	❑	❑	❑	❑	❑

I consciously redirect or limit criticism and/or complaints:

Never	Infrequently	Rarely	Regularly	Frequently	Usually	Always
❑	❑	❑	❑	❑	❑	❑

Describe your attitude about complaints:

____

____

____

____

____

____

Discuss a way to lend support, but to redirect an unproductive complaint.

____
____
____
____
____
____

Action Guide—25

Rule of 48

Carve out 2/48THS of your day every day for one year to focus energy on something you want to change, add, or enhance.

12:00 a.m. ____
12:30 a.m. ____
01:00 a.m. ____
01:30 a.m. ____
02:00 a.m. ____
02:30 a.m. ____
03:00 a.m. ____
03:30 a.m. ____
04:00 a.m. ____
04:30 a.m. ____
05:00 a.m. ____
05:30 a.m. ____
06:00 a.m.
06:30 a.m. ____
07:00 a.m. ____
07:30 a.m. ____
08:00 a.m. ____
08:30 a.m. ____
09:00 a.m. ____
09:30 a.m. ____
10:00 a.m. ____
10:30 a.m. ____

11:00 a.m. ____

11:30 a.m. ____

12:00 p.m. ____

12:30 p.m. ____

01:00 p.m. ____

01:30 p.m. ____

02:00 p.m. ____

02:30 p.m. ____

03:00 p.m. ____

03:30 p.m. ____

04:00 p.m. ____

04:30 p.m. ____

05:00 p.m. ____

05:30 p.m. ____

06:00 p.m. ____

06:30 p.m. ____

07:00 p.m. ____

07:30 p.m. ____

08:00 p.m. ____

08:30 p.m.____

09:00 p.m.____

09:30 p.m. ____

10:00 p.m. ____

10:30 p.m. ____

11:00 p.m. ____

11:30 p.m. ____

Action Guide 26

MOMENTUM

Momentum is a physical property in which mass and motion equal velocity. A big idea or a big shift in habits begins small. As you add your focus with persistence, it picks up speed.

A sense of urgency fuels momentum.

Once the size of your project, habit change, or big idea has reached critical mass, the momentum is almost self-sustaining. It takes much less energy to keep it going—and a huge counter-energy from the opposite direction to halt it.

Describe a defining event in your life when you used momentum resourcefully.

Describe a defining event in your life in which you used momentum non-resourcefully.

Action Guide 27

Name one big dream in relationship to your family that you have wanted but not yet set aside time to accomplish.

What story have you told yourself to stop you from setting the time aside?

____

____

____

____

____

____

Name one big dream in relation to your career that you have wanted but have not yet set aside time to accomplish?

____

____

____

____

____

____

What story have you told yourself to stop you from setting the time aside?

____

____

____

____

____

____

Action Guide 28

PERSISTENCE

Persistence is the habit of going on resolutely or stubbornly in spite of opposition, importunity, or warning, to be insistent in repetition that goes past a usual, expected or normal time.

The Four Steps of Persistence

- a definite purpose backed by a burning desire for its fulfillment
- a definite plan, expressed in continuous action

- a mind closed tightly against all negative and discouraging influences, including negative suggestions of relatives, colleagues, and friends
- a friendly alliance with one or more people who will encourage one to follow through with both plan and purpose (a mastermind group).

In which areas of your life are you most persistent? Rank the following from 1 to 9 (1 is the area of your life in which you are most persistent).

Relationships with your spouse/significant other______
Relationships with family______
Relationships (excluding family)______
Business/career advancement______
Financial freedom______
Personal time______
Spiritual life______
Contribution______
Knowledge/growth______

In which areas could you benefit most if you were more persistent? Why?

____

____

____

____

____

> There may be no heroic connotation to the word persistence, but the quality is to the character of man what carbon is to steel.
> —Napoleon Hill

Action Guide 29

Most people will exert far more effort to <u>avoid pain</u> than to <u>gain pleasure</u>.

Using the same categories / associations we used in Guide 24, circle which area of your **persistence** is motivated primarily by your desire to <u>avoid pain</u> (**AP**) or <u>gain pleasure</u> (**GP**)

Relationships with your spouse/significant other AP GP
Relationships with your family AP GP
Relationships (excluding family) AP GP
Business/career advancement AP GP
Financial freedom AP GP
Personal time AP GP
Spiritual life AP GP
Contribution AP GP
Knowledge/growth AP GP

What did you discover about yourself in this process?

What category do you most want to improve?
List several steps you can take immediately and reinforce with persistence over the next forty days.

> The secret of success is learning how to use pain and pleasure instead of having pain and pleasure use you. If you do that, you are in control of your life. If you don't, life controls you.
> —Anthony Robbins

Action Guide 30

PROCRASTINATION

Procrastination is the habit of intentionally putting off something that you know should be done. It is the ultimate form of irresponsibility.

PROCRASTINATION IS THE ANTITHESIS OF PERSISTENCE, AND IT STIFLES YOUR SENSE OF URGENCY.

Procrastination is fueled by fear and avoidance of pain. When we procrastinate, we usually cause ourselves more pain in the end.

Train yourself to notice the thought processes that lead to procrastination. When you notice yourself procrastinating, recognize the pain you have linked to doing the thing you know you should do. You have associated more pain with doing what needs to be done than you have to avoiding the work. A warning signal should immediately go off in your head. Begin to consciously link more pain to procrastination and massive pleasure to completion.

> Doing at once what needs to be done will
> increase the possibility of success—
> Leland Val Van De Walle Wall

Action Guide 31

Rate yourself from 0 to 10 in how you see yourself most of the time.

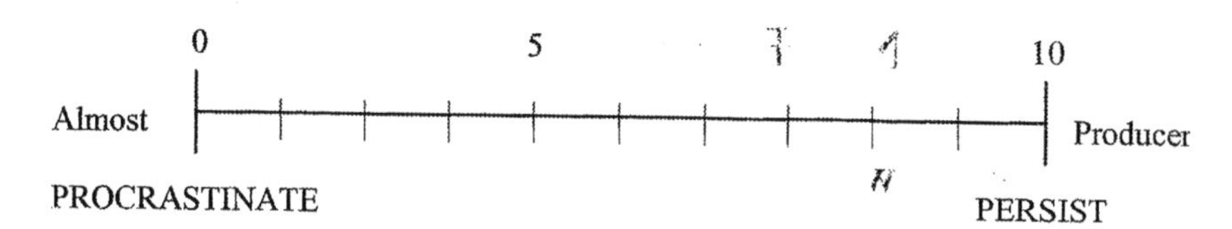

In what area(s) of your life do you procrastinate most? Why?

____

____

____

Do you have certain activities or behaviors in which you engage when you procrastinate?
If so, list them.

What is the usual outcome of your procrastination?

Describe what you will do to abort procrastination when you notice thoughts and/or activities that represent procrastination for you.

Action Guide 32

Practical Solutions for Managing Procrastination

Solution 1—Do the Worst First

Tackle first the thing you most resist. Whether it is a conversation, a report, or a pile of mail, the thing you dread most drains the most energy and keeps you in the procrastination cycle most solidly. To unstick that negative energy, get the worst thing out of the way.

Solution 2—Divide and Conquer

Break tasks into small parts. With tedious jobs like catching up on mail, commit to handling three to five letters per day. To get started on a report, commit to writing one page per day. To learn a new computer program, commit to spending thirty minutes per day, five days a week.

Solution 3—Create Time Blocks

Get up one hour earlier, use thirty minutes of your lunch hour every day, and stay up one hour later at night (not in front of the TV). Reserve that time for a specific job you want to complete.

* Note: If you have a three-hour chunk of time in your schedule, tackle a bigger task rather than focusing your energy on several smaller jobs. Use these time blocks to focus on things that will create a bigger future.

Solution 4—Circle in toward Completion

Move from the general to the specifics. If you have a mound of paperwork to handle, sort it into a few broad, manageable categories. Later in the process, you can deal with each piece of paper.

* Note: As you get down to handling each piece of paper, handle each piece only once. Resist setting it aside again and again. Each time you pick it up, you have to read it, *wasting time.*

Solution 5—Start Anywhere

When you are so overwhelmed that you do not know where to begin, be arbitrary and start anywhere. **The secret to getting ahead is getting started**. If the way you began is not the best way to continue, you can always make whatever adjustments will be more effective.

Solution 6—Planning Action

When a project is so huge and unwieldy that you seem to run in circles every time you try to tackle it, write down the action elements necessary to complete the project. As you review these elements, you will find that some elements naturally precede others. A type of blueprint of action will unfold for you as you take on the various elements.

> No idleness, no laziness, no procrastination;
> never put off till tomorrow what you can do today.
> —Lord Chesterfield

Printed in the United States
By Bookmasters